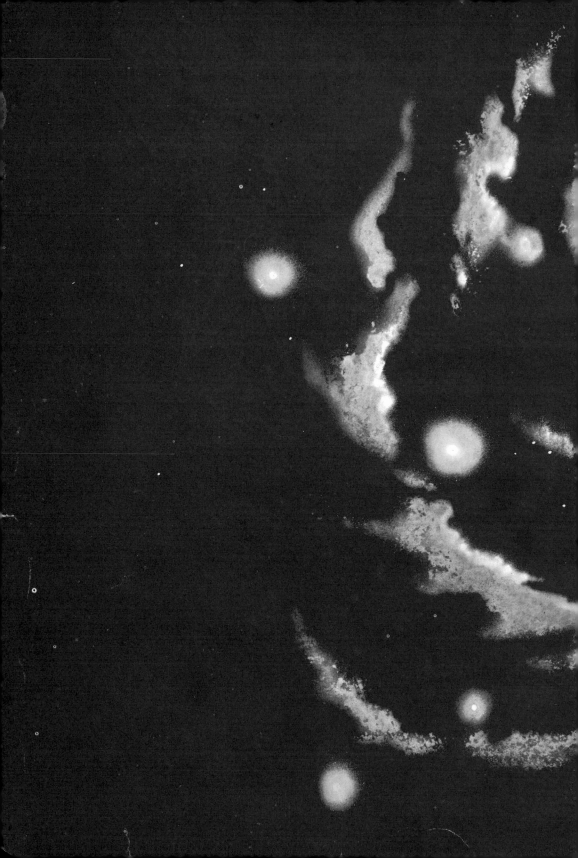

All About THE PLANETS

Seen from far out in space, Earth would seem one of the least exciting planets in our solar system. Yet it is a very special planet because it supports human life. It is also our observation station for the other eight planets.

   Where did the sun and its planets come from? Are there other planets in solar systems like ours? If so, do these planets support life? Patricia Lauber tells what astronomers have learned—and are learning—in answer to these exciting questions.

ALL ABOUT

The Planets

By PATRICIA LAUBER

Foreword by Harlow Shapley

Illustrations by Arthur Renshaw

allabout
books

RANDOM
HOUSE
NEW YORK

For helpful suggestions about the illustrations, grateful acknowledgment is made to Lloyd Motz, Associate Professor of Astronomy, Columbia University.

Contents

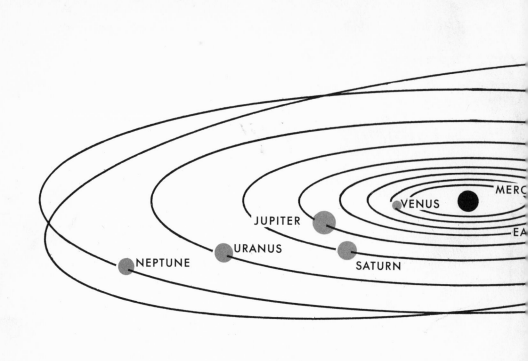

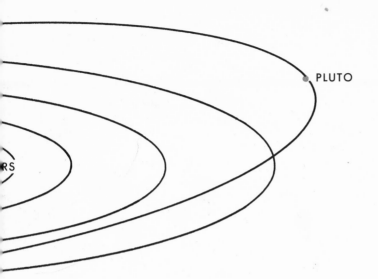

PLUTO

Symbols for the Planets

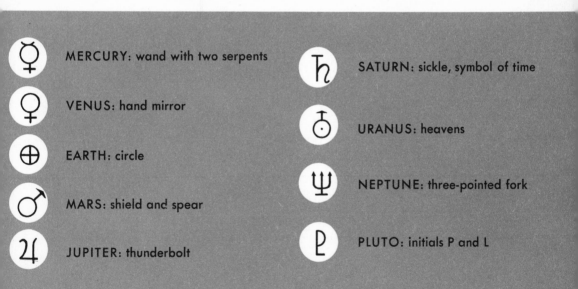

MERCURY: wand with two serpents

VENUS: hand mirror

EARTH: circle

MARS: shield and spear

JUPITER: thunderbolt

SATURN: sickle, symbol of time

URANUS: heavens

NEPTUNE: three-pointed fork

PLUTO: initials P and L

Foreword

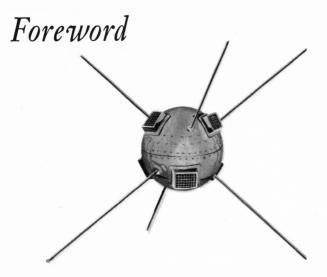

For many years, we who ponder astronomical matters were rather indifferent to the nearby parts of the universe. We were exploring the chemistry of stars and the motions of great galaxies. But the launching of artificial satellites has focused attention on the family of planets that orbit our sun. Becoming "space-minded," we naturally look with interest at the little moon and the nearby planets. And we consider them scarcely more difficult for exploration and conquest than the Antarctic continent was a century ago.

In this thoroughly enjoyable book on planets, Patricia Lauber assists the curious and ambitious reader by providing a reliable background for planetary travels. Written in a very attractive style and with smooth and logical argument, her volume is both a beginner's text and a guidebook. She reports on what is known—and what is not known. In fact, some readers may be surprised to discover in this book how many unknowns still challenge the student of the local planetary system.

For example, there may or may not be undiscovered planets beyond Pluto. There is as yet no accepted solution of the problem of asteroids—those curious fragments of a planet which once existed, or which could not exist because of the disturbing presence of nearby giant planet Jupiter. The origin of the solar system is also among the unknowns, although an origin from a contracting cloud of gas is increasingly credible as we learn more about interstellar gas and the distribution of chemical elements in the sun and earth. Another unknown is the surface structure of the outer planets.

Miss Lauber points out that the sun is mostly hydrogen and helium. In small part it is composed of heavier atoms that were synthesized in the hot interiors of giant stars that later exploded as super-novae.

The probability of life, of the sort we recognize, on Mars and Venus is treated by Miss Lauber with the caution that is proper in these days of rockets and satellite telescopes. Certainly we shall have stronger evidence in a few years and then be able to say whether the changing seasonal colors on Mars are due to vegetational responses, or are just the result of sand storms on our planetary neighbor.

HARLOW SHAPLEY

Harvard University

All About THE PLANETS

I

The Cloud

Long, long ago a vast cloud floated in space. It was big beyond imagining—probably trillions of miles in diameter—and it was made of gas and dust. In the beginning, the tiny particles that composed the cloud were spread very thin.

But the particles were moving a little. They were being pushed together by the pressure of starlight, and they also tended to attract one another. Very slowly they drifted over huge distances, swirling in toward the center of the cloud. After a billion years had passed, the cloud had shrunk to half its original size.

This smaller cloud was more dense; that is, its particles were closer together. As a result, the forces of gravity among them increased. They moved faster and faster, becoming hotter and hotter.

While this material streamed inward, the cloud was spinning, rather like the funnel of a gigantic whirlpool. In time, parts of it collapsed toward the center, forming a huge ball of gas. And parts of it flattened into a spinning disk that circled the center.

Within the disk of gas and dust, other smaller whirlpools formed. The dust particles, which were heavier, settled toward the centers of the eddies. Small particles collided with larger particles and were added to the bodies of the larger ones. The collisions, which created heat, continued. At the heart of the eddies, masses of glowing hot material took shape. They grew larger and larger. And all the while they were circling the great ball of gas at the center of the cloud.

The ball of gas had grown and grown. Under enormous pressure, it began to glow, to send out heat and light. And so a new star was born, the star that men would one day call their sun. Traveling around it in widely spaced orbits were the planets. Some were only millions of miles from the sun. Others were several billion miles away, out where the edge of the great flat disk had been.

In much this way, most scientists believe, our solar system came into being almost five billion years ago. The sun was born of a cloud of gas and dust. The planets formed in the flat ring of leftover material that circled the sun.

When this first stage ended, the newly formed planets were swinging around the newly glowing sun. Perhaps at that time the planets all looked very much alike. And in many ways they *were* alike. Yet one planet—the third one out from the sun—turned out to be different. This was the planet Earth, which long after became our home.

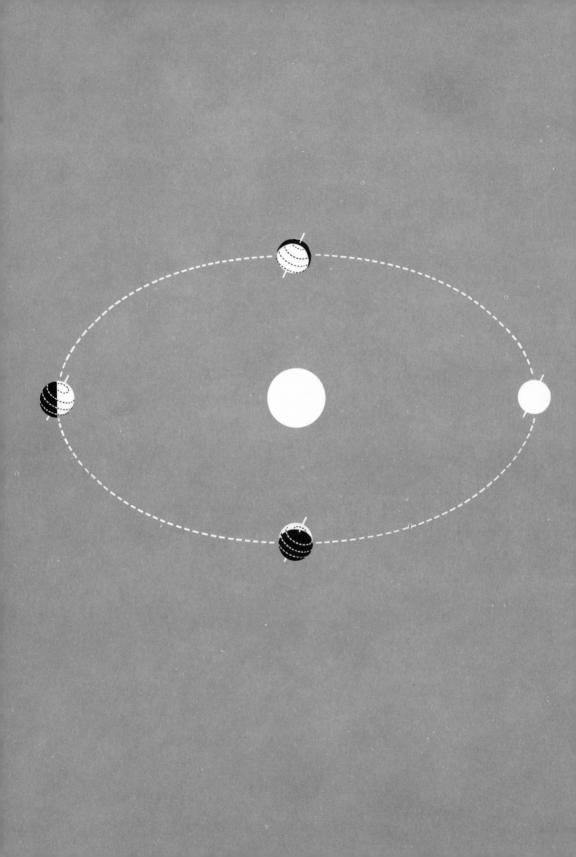

2

Earth, Our Home Planet

Seen from far out in space, Earth would seem one of the least exciting planets in our solar system. As planets go, the earth is fairly small. And from a distance there would be nothing very eye-catching about it. It isn't a giant, like Jupiter. It isn't circled by beautiful rings, like Saturn. It isn't red, like Mars. It has only one moon, compared with Jupiter's twelve or Saturn's nine.

Yet a closer view of the earth—say, from a million miles away—would show it as a very interesting planet. Earth would be marked with brilliant white patches; large areas of green; here and there a patch of dusky red; and vast areas of inky black that would occasionally give off blinding flashes.

The white patches are Earth's polar icecaps and its clouds. The dusky red marks deserts. The dark areas are our oceans, which would appear black except when they reflected the sun's light. The greens are plants, ranging from the pale green of young crops to the dark green of northern forests.

The greens would give the first hint that the earth is more than just interesting. Watched over a period of months, they could be seen to change. Every spring a great wave of green spreads poleward from the equator. Within the wave of green there are other changes. Pale greens darken, then turn yellow or red-brown. For a few months, some greens vanish completely. The area that was green appears brown-gray or white. Then, once more, pale green appears and darkens. These changing colors are a sign of widespread, vigorous plant life. This alone makes Earth a remarkable planet.

A still closer view—perhaps a thousand miles away—would show the planet to be very remarkable indeed. When the shadows of night fell upon certain parts of the earth, the lights of great cities could be seen going on. This is a sign of intelligent life, and it makes the earth unique. No other planet in our solar system shows signs of supporting intelligent life.

The planet Earth is basically nothing more than a ball of rock and metal surrounded by an envelope of water and air, which speeds around the sun at 67,000 miles an hour. Yet there are many things about this small planet that make it just right for supporting life.

To start with, there's the sun we circle. Compared with other stars, our sun is not particularly big or brilliant. But from our point of view, it is exceptionally fine.

Our sun is a steady producer of the light and heat required

by life on earth. Most stars are not such steady producers of light and heat. Some change often, dimming and then growing brighter. Some flare up suddenly, turning loose a blast of withering heat. Our sun does none of these things. Its output of light and heat hardly varies at all.

Our sun's gravitational field is also steady. It keeps the earth revolving steadily around the sun in its orbit. If the sun's gravitational field were not steady, the earth might be tossed about like a ping-pong ball on a stormy sea. Sometimes we would be pulled too close to the sun for comfort. Other times we'd find ourselves too far away. Great changes in our climate would occur each time our distance changed. This would make many—perhaps all—kinds of life impossible. Living things depend on a regular climate.

Earth's distance from the sun is also ideal. On the average, we are about 93 million miles from the sun. (Scientists call this our "mean distance," saying "mean" instead of "average.") We receive just the right amount of heat and light to support our kind of life.

The way our planet moves around the sun is also very important to life.

As it revolves around the sun, the earth is also rotating. That is, it spins on its axis—an imaginary line running through the North and South Poles. It completes one spin in just a little less than 24 hours. By the time the earth has made 365 rotations, it has completed one trip around the sun. For this reason, we say our year has 365 days.

The year also has seasons. The seasons result from the tilt

of the earth's axis. Winter comes to the Northern Hemisphere when our part of the earth is tipped away from the sun. Summer comes when it is tipped toward the sun.

Earth's spin and the tilt of its axis make our planet an extremely pleasant place to live. Every part of the earth gets some sunlight. Only the polar regions—which receive weak, slanting rays of sunlight—are very cold. Only the equator —which receives strong, direct rays—is very hot. Most parts of the earth are kept at bearable temperatures. The seasons change, giving each part a chance to become hotter or colder. In the same way, day brings warmth and, a few hours later, night brings coolness.

Our small planet has other good things about it, too. One of the most important is the atmosphere, the blanket of air several hundred miles deep that envelopes the earth.

We could not live without the atmosphere. It is the air we breathe. The atmosphere is thin enough to let the sun's light and heat pass through. It is thick enough to shield us from the dangerous rays of the sun, which it filters out.

The atmosphere is held captive by the earth's gravity. If gravity were only a fourth or a fifth as strong, our atmosphere would long ago have escaped into space. Earth would be a barren, airless globe of rock and metal, like Mercury or the moon.

Earth's atmosphere is unique in the solar system. Only Mars and Venus have atmospheres that resemble ours. But they cannot support life as we know it.

The mixture of gases in Earth's atmosphere is good, too. The mixture is about four-fifths nitrogen and one-fifth oxygen, with traces of argon, carbon dioxide, helium, hydrogen, and several other gases. The carbon dioxide is required by plants. The oxygen—called "free oxygen" because it is not combined with other elements—is what men and animals require. To the best of our knowledge, there is not much free oxygen on any planet except Earth.

So in every way—its steady sun, its regular orbit, its seasons, its short days and nights, its atmosphere—Earth is, for us, the pleasantest planet imaginable. It is the only one in our solar system that could support our kind of life.

In a way, of course, this would have to be so. Since life evolved here, it's only natural that the earth seems ideal to us. And we can go one step further. It's also true that part of the earth's pleasantness has been created by the living things that developed here. For the earth as we know it today did not spring into existence ready-made.

Nobody knows what the earth was like at the time of its

The Planet Earth

mean diameter	7,913 miles
mean distance from sun	92,900,000 miles
mean speed of revolution	67,000 miles per hour
length of year	365¼ days
length of day	23 hours, 56 minutes
number of moons	1

birth four or five billion years ago. But many scientists think that it was wrapped in a dense cloud of atmosphere, which was later driven away. Underneath this ball of clouds, the young earth may have been extremely hot. It may have been so hot that the solid material took the form of gas. As the earth cooled, the gases condensed into liquid that later solidified into rock and metal. The cooling took hundreds of millions of years, during which the earth bubbled and spewed gases into the air. Beneath this new atmosphere of hot gases, a thin solid crust began to form on the young and cooling earth.

At some time during the cooling off, the air temperature dropped to a point where rain occurred. It was rain that fell only in the sky. When raindrops neared the earth's cooling but still hot crust, they evaporated. Steam rose into the atmosphere, condensed, and turned again to rain. Only when the crust cooled still more did the first rains strike the earth's surface. Over a long period of time, steady, heavy rains formed rivers, lakes, and oceans on the young planet.

By the time it was two billion years old, the earth had changed greatly.

It now had a cool, solid crust. Most of the crust was probably covered by a deep ocean. Land areas—if there were any—consisted of rock. The soil lying in cracks between the rocks was ground-up stone. The oceans, the rocks, the soil, the rivers were all barren and lifeless.

Surrounding the earth was an atmosphere of poisonous gases. Most likely they included ammonia and methane; methane is also known as marsh gas. The ammonia was a compound of nitrogen and hydrogen. The methane was a compound of carbon and hydrogen.

By this time the atmosphere was thin enough so that some sunlight could penetrate it and reach the surface of the earth. The sunlight fell upon scenes of terrible violence. The earth was still growing, catching up material from space. Giant meteors pelted the young planet, blasting craters in its crust. Thunderstorms raged across the surface. Volcanoes exploded. Mighty forces deep within the earth squeezed and folded the surface, forcing up mountains and continents.

That scene set the stage for life.

Modern scientists believe that life will appear wherever conditions remain favorable for a very long time. And they say that conditions on the earth two billion years ago were just right for life to begin.

Scientists do not know—and may never know—precisely how life began. But they suppose that something like this may have happened.

Heat and lightning acted on certain gases in the atmosphere, creating amino acids, which are the building blocks of living matter. The amino acids were carried by raindrops into the warm ocean. In time they combined into more complex structures. Then—somewhere, somehow, sometime—a piece of living protein was produced.

What happened after that is a whole story in itself. For our purposes, it is enough to know that in the lifeless ocean of the young earth, life was probably born. From that first life all other life is descended.

The development of the first living molecule may have taken a few million years or a billion years or even more. The earliest living molecules may have continued in the same form for a billion years, or only a few million. But eventually a great change took place.

A molecule began to capture energy from sunlight. It used the energy to make food out of chemicals. The process of using sunlight to make food is called photosynthesis, and it is the way modern plants make their food.

The first plants were probably tiny and slow-growing, though this is just a guess. We can be sure of only one thing about them. The most successful ones became the ancestors of our green plants; they established the pattern of plant life we know today. The plants absorbed carbon dioxide, a compound of carbon and oxygen. With energy from sunlight and the magic of chlorophyll, they broke up the carbon dioxide. They used the carbon to make food, and they released the oxygen The oxygen returned to the water. After a time it was drawn into the atmosphere.

The new, food-making plants multiplied and spread. Day after day, they took in carbon dioxide, used the carbon, and released free oxygen. As a result, the atmosphere very slowly began to change. The amount of free oxygen in it increased. And oxygen is chemically very active.

Oxygen attacked the methane in the air, changing it to carbon dioxide and water. Oxygen attacked ammonia, combining with the hydrogen in it to form water and releasing the nitrogen. After a while, there were no more gases for the oxygen to attack. It simply began to accumulate in the atmosphere.

The atmosphere became what it is today—chiefly a mixture of nitrogen and oxygen, with just a trace of carbon dioxide and other gases. Then another great change took place. The animal age began.

The first animals did not even vaguely resemble dogs or horses or tigers. Like the early plants, they were just large molecules. The chief difference between them and the plants was the way each group made food.

The plants drew energy from sunlight, broke down carbon dioxide, used the carbon, and released the oxygen.

The animals ate plants and, inhaling air, used oxygen as fuel to "burn" their food. Exhaling, they released carbon dioxide into the air.

Animal life today, including man, still does precisely that. All animal life depends on green plants. The plants are food; the oxygen freed by plants is the fuel needed to "burn" the food.

So, out of the young earth's atmosphere and ocean came life. Plant life changed the atmosphere. Animal life began. Plants and animals changed the land as they learned to live on it. Higher forms of life developed from lower ones. Earth became more and more the world we know today—a small but remarkable planet which is our home and from which we look out into the sky, seeking to know what lies beyond us.

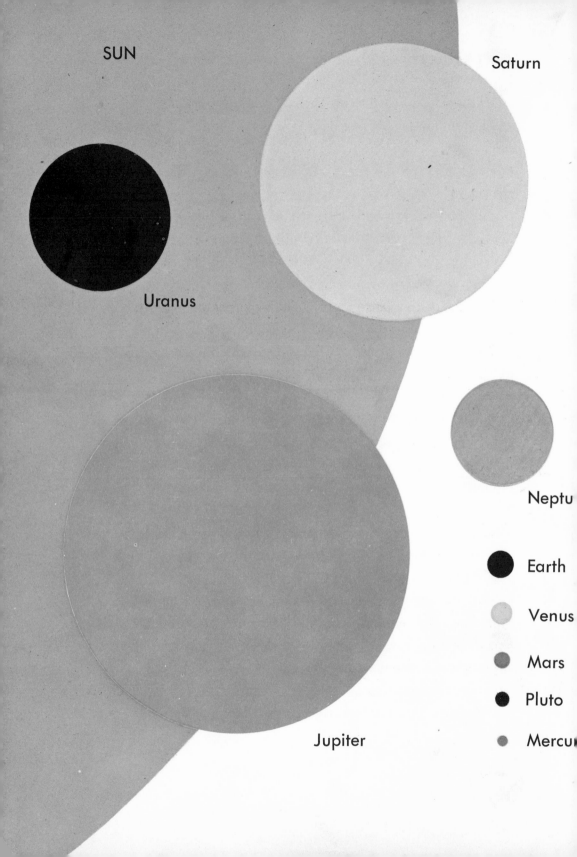

3

The Five Wanderers

Probably from earliest times men turned their eyes upward with awe, marveling at the sun that filled the sky by day and the stars that came by night. Then, watching and remembering, they realized that there was a regularity to what happened in the heavens. They began to make use of this. Hunters used the stars as a guide to find their way home at night. Much later, when men began to plant crops, they noticed that certain groups of stars—constellations—appeared in the sky at a particular time each year. The appearances became a guide to the seasons: time to plant or time to harvest. Still later, men learned to reckon time through what they saw in the heavens. So, at some time long ago, the oldest of sciences, astronomy, was born out of a need to know the skies.

As ancient astronomers mapped the night skies, they found five stars that were different from the others.

Most stars always held the same position in the same constellation. The five did not. Instead, they wandered through a certain band of constellations. They were different in one other way, too. While the fixed stars shone with a twinkling light, the five shone with a light that was steadier.

The ancient Greeks, the world's first great scientists, gave the five strange stars a special name. The five were known as *planets,* meaning "wanderers." These five were the planets we call Mercury, Venus, Mars, Jupiter, and Saturn.

Working without telescopes, the Greeks knew very little about the planets beyond what their eyes told them. But they had carefully plotted the paths of the planets through the night sky. The results created a very great problem. The planets would not fit into the system that astronomers used to explain the workings of the universe.

The ancients believed that the earth stood still at the center of the universe, while all the heavenly bodies revolved around it. Their reasoning is not hard to understand. Why should anyone think that this solid, stable earth was moving? Here it was—the same, day after day, beneath men's feet. It did not tilt. It did not roll about. On the other hand, anyone could see that the sun, the moon, and the stars were all moving. At various rates, they traveled across the sky, vanished, and returned. Clearly, men thought, the earth stood still and all things moved around it.

A few scientists, some 2400 years ago, did glimpse the truth. They believed that a central fire stood at the center of the universe. They believed that everything, including the earth, moved around the fire. But to most people this idea was ridiculous. Earth was obviously the center of the universe.

Astronomers explained that the universe consisted of a series of crystal spheres, one within another. At the center of the spheres was the earth. Beyond it, each in a separate sphere, lay the moon, Mercury, Venus, the sun, Mars, Jupiter, and Saturn. Beyond these lay a large, dark sphere to which the stars were firmly attached. All the spheres revolved around the earth.

The system worked quite well for the moon, the sun, and the stars. All of them appeared regularly and moved regularly across the sky. But it did not work for the planets. Instead of

Ancient men thought that the stars and planets moved around the earth.

Saturn
Jupiter
Mars
Sun
Venus
Mercury
Moon

EARTH

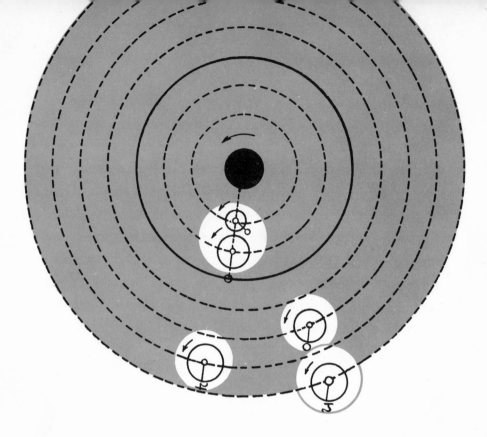

Ptolemy believed that the planets moved around the earth in a complicated system of circles.

moving steadily forward, the wanderers sometimes reversed their courses and moved backward for a short time. How could this happen if each planet was attached to a perfectly round sphere and circling the earth?

The first astronomer to attack the problem was Ptolemy of Alexandria. He explained the motions of the planets this way. Each planet, he said, is moving around the earth in the circle of its sphere. But each planet also has a second motion. It is moving in a small circle that lies on the edge of the large circle.

That is, the planet is moving around the circumference of a small circle; the center of the small circle moves around the circumference of the large circle.

There the matter rested for more than a thousand years. The great age of learning had come to an end and was not reborn until the 1200's.

At that time manuscripts from the ancient world found their way into the hands of Church scholars in Europe. The scholars were stunned by the wealth of information in these books. With great enthusiasm they took over the scientific ideas of Greece and Alexandria, including the belief that the earth was the center of the universe. It was an extremely pleasing idea. For if the earth was the center of the universe and man was master of the earth, then man was master of the universe.

Astronomers tried to explain the motions of the planets.

They observed that the planets did not always move at the same speed. How could this be so if they were all moving around the earth in perfect circles? Astronomers tried to solve the problem by giving the earth a position slightly off center in their diagrams. If the earth was not at the exact center of the universe, then the speed of the planets would appear to vary.

A still worse problem was the one Ptolemy had attacked. Usually the planets are seen moving eastward among the stars. Yet the time comes when a planet seems to turn around and move westward. How could this be explained?

Astronomers adopted Ptolemy's solution. But careful observation kept turning up things that couldn't be explained by a small circle on a large circle. So astronomers kept adding more circles. Finally they had an enormous collection of circles upon circles upon circles. And it still didn't explain the motions of the planets.

The man who cut through this problem was the Polish astronomer Copernicus. He worked out a new system, placing the sun at the center of the universe.

This was a daring idea. At the time, an attack on an earth-centered universe was considered an attack on the Church. So Copernicus hesitated to publish his theory. Instead he made it part of a long and technical book. The book was not published until 1543, when Copernicus was on his deathbed. Buried in the long book were three very important ideas:

(1) The sun, not the earth, is the center of the universe.

(2) All the planets, including the earth, move around the sun.

(3) Earth spins on its axis once every 24 hours. It is the earth's rotation that makes the sun and stars appear to move around us.

These ideas helped to explain the strange wanderings of the planets. Mars, for example, does not really move backward. It just *appears* to because both the earth and Mars are moving.

Copernicus had expected his book to create an uproar, but it went almost unnoticed. It was so technical that very few people could read and understand it.

Among the people who did were two great astronomers, the Italian Galileo and the German Johannes Kepler. Galileo struck the next blow for a sun-centered universe.

In 1609 Galileo heard that a Dutch spectacle-maker had

accidentally invented a spyglass. Galileo immediately set about building one for himself. In the winter of 1609-10 he became the first man to turn a telescope on the night sky.

The moon, the stars, the planets—there was so much to see that Galileo hardly knew how to spend his time. He noted a difference in the appearance of the planets and the stars. The planets, he reported, "show their globes perfectly round . . . looking like little moons, spherical and flooded all over with light. The fixed stars . . . have the aspect of blazes whose rays vibrate about them."

Turning his telescope on Jupiter, he discovered that the planet had moons revolving around it. Here before his eyes was a miniature solar system. The moons revolved around Jupiter just as Copernicus had said the planets revolve around the sun.

The telescope showed Galileo that Venus went through phases, like the moon. This was further evidence that Copernicus was right. The phases could occur only if Venus was moving around the sun and was closer than Earth to the sun.

Galileo's findings caused a tremendous uproar and got him into serious trouble. But the truth about man's place in the universe was beginning to emerge. Once started, it could not be stopped.

Just about that time, Kepler announced the first of his three great laws that explain the movement of the planets about the sun. Kepler destroyed the old and false idea that planets move in circles. He showed that planets move in oval paths called ellipses. He also proved that the speed of a planet does vary.

As a planet nears the sun, it speeds up; as it draws away from the sun, it slows down.

And some years later, Isaac Newton explained why planets travel around the sun in orbits. A planet's movement results from the balance of two forces. One is inertia—the tendency to keep moving forever in a straight line. The other is gravity —the pull of the sun. Without the sun's gravity, the planet would fly off into space. Without inertia, it would be drawn into the fiery mass of the sun. The balance of the two forces keeps the planet moving around the sun in its orbit.

The work of Copernicus, Galileo, Kepler, and Newton marked the start of modern astronomy. Copernicus and Galileo led the way in showing that man is not the center of the universe or even of the solar system. Kepler and Newton discovered the basic laws that govern the movements of the planets. Once this groundwork had been laid, discoveries came at a staggering rate.

Galileo observed that Venus, like the moon, goes through phases.

Today we know that our solar system contains nine planets that whirl through space around the sun. A planet is not, as the ancients thought, a kind of wandering star. A star is a fiery furnace of gases that generates light and heat. A planet is a solid body held captive by the sun. It does not generate light and heat. It receives light and heat from the sun, and it shines by reflected light. When a planet is far away from the sun, it cannot reflect much light because it does not receive much. That is why the outer planets appear dim to us. They are not nearly so bright as a much more distant star which generates its own light.

Today, too, everyone knows that the earth is a planet. It is special because it supports human life. But in every other way it is simply one of nine planets, all of which obey the same laws. These laws make the solar system a most orderly place.

All major bodies in the solar system move in the same direction. As seen from the north side, the sun spins on its axis in a

counter-clockwise direction. So do the planets. And they move counter-clockwise around the sun.

Except for Pluto, all the planets move in nearly the same plane in space. This is shown in the drawing of the solar system at the beginning of this book.

Every planet's orbit is an ellipse. Some of these orbits come very close to being circles, but they are still ellipses. The planets travel around their orbits at varying speeds that follow a pattern: the closer a planet is to the sun, the faster it travels.

The telescope has shown astronomers that the planets fall into two distinct classes, determined by size and density. Density is a measure of the amount of matter in a body of a certain volume. (A baseball and a tennis ball, for example, are about the same size. But the baseball is much more dense: there is more matter packed into its volume.)

The first class consists of small, solid planets—Mercury, Venus, Earth, Mars, and Pluto. Earth is the largest of these. All have a mean density several times that of water.

The second class is made up of the giant planets—Jupiter, Saturn, Uranus, Neptune. The largest of these, Jupiter, has a diameter almost eleven times greater than the earth's. Neptune, the smallest, has a diameter four times that of the earth. However, the densities of the four giants are low. This means that they must be made in part of gas or liquid.

One of the most striking things about our solar system is its "emptiness"—the vast gulfs of space that lie between the planets. On the average, Mercury is almost 36 million miles

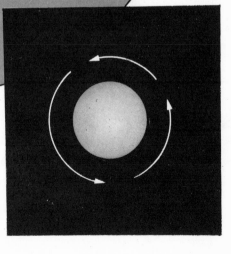

If you looked at the solar system from the
North Star, you would see the sun and
the planets all spinning counter-clockwise.
And you would see the planets moving
counter-clockwise around the sun.

from the sun. Pluto is a hundred times farther away. Between these two are the seven other planets. The distances are so great and the planets so small that it is almost impossible to make an accurate model of the solar system. If the earth is made the size of a ping-pong ball, then Pluto must be placed ten miles away.

Even so, astronomers have learned to probe these great distances. They have found planets that are invisible to the unaided eye. They can tell you the temperatures on Mars. They can tell you about gases in the atmosphere of Venus.

The most important tool of the astronomer is the telescope, which magnifies a distant object and thus makes it seem closer. As Galileo discovered, the telescope reveals objects too dim for the unaided eye to see. But since his time, telescopes have grown greatly in power and size. Astronomers often couple the telescope with a camera. They use light-sensitive plates to measure the brightness and track the paths of faint pinpoints of light.

To measure temperature, astronomers use a device called a thermocouple, along with a telescope. A highly sensitive thermocouple can detect heat from a candle three miles away.

To analyze light gathered by the telescope, astronomers use a spectroscope. It works on this principle. When a beam of light passes through a prism, it spreads out into a rainbow of colors. We call this the *spectrum*; the plural of the word is *spectra*. Suppose a beam of light from a planet or a star is passed through the spectroscope. When the colors are widely spread, the spectra show thousands of lines, both bright and dark. Each line has a meaning. For example, a bright yellow-orange line in a certain position shows glowing sodium in the light source. Other lines show hydrogen, helium, ammonia, and so on. If certain lines are not sharp but fuzzy, they indicate that the planet or star is spinning rapidly.

With these tools and others, astronomers have reached out from the earth into space. They have gathered information at a dizzying pace. They have made discoveries undreamed of three hundred years ago.

Much of what they have learned about the members of our solar family is summed up in this book. But many tantalizing questions remain without answers because we cannot see well enough. Even the most powerful telescope shows almost nothing of dimly lighted Pluto. And our view of brighter objects is blurred by the earth's very atmosphere.

Looking through the atmosphere with a strong telescope is like studying a distant street scene through a window whose glass is wavy and slightly dirty. No matter how you strain your eyes, you cannot make out certain details. You think you see a cat, but it just might be a dog, and someone else sees it as a duck.

However, the next great breakthrough in astronomy lies just ahead, as rockets and man-made satellites carry the astronomers' instruments into space. From probes of the nearer planets, from satellite observatories orbiting high above the earth, we can gather information unblurred by the atmosphere.

Finally, the day will come when men set out in rocket ships. The ancient science of astronomy will become a kind of geography as men explore what today we can only imperfectly see. And the first new world to be explored will be the moon, the satellite of our planet Earth.

The moon, moving around the earth at
a mean distance of 238,857 miles, is our
closest neighbor in space.

4

The Moon, Earth's Satellite

A ship caught up in a gigantic waterspout is carried to the moon. There the voyagers find a war going on. The men of the moon are fighting the men of the sun over the right to colonize Venus.

That is the beginning of the world's first known science-fiction story. Called *True History*, it was written by Lucian of Samos around the year 160.

The moon was a natural subject for the first science fiction because it seemed very special to people of ancient times. Anyone could see that the moon, unlike the stars and planets, was big. And it had markings on its face. Many ancient scientists believed these markings outlined seas and continents. This suggested that the moon was an inhabited world, like the earth.

Though no one today thinks the moon is inhabited, it is still "special" in the eyes of scientists.

31

Astronomers point out that our moon is a very big satellite for a small planet. There are bigger moons in the solar system. But no other moon is so big in proportion to the size of its planet. The moon's diameter is more than a fourth of the earth's.

The moon is also our near neighbor. It is only a quarter of a million miles away, which is very close as distances in the solar system go. Because of its nearness, astronomers know a great deal about the moon. Since the invention of the telescope, ten generations of them have studied it and thoroughly mapped its face.

Space scientists also look on the moon as special. Its size and distance mean we can hit it with a rocket pretty easily. Perhaps that is the most important thing about the moon today. It gives us a chance to practice "at home" before reaching out for the planets.

In time, we may well use the moon as a take-off point for journeys to distant planets. The reason is that the moon's gravity is considerably lower than the earth's. For example, a spaceship would have to attain a speed of 26,000 miles an hour to escape the earth and coast to Venus. Escaping from the moon on a trip to Venus, the same ship would require a speed of only 7,000 miles an hour.

For these reasons, the first dream of space travel will be the first one to come true. Our first trip will be to the moon. But voyagers from the earth will travel by rocket, not by water-spout. And we won't find moon men fighting sun men.

On arrival we shall find a small, dead, airless world.

Some astronomers say the moon is completely airless. Others

think it may have a very thin atmosphere—between 1/10,000 and 1/1,000,000 as dense as ours. From our point of view, such a thin atmosphere would be little better than none. We could not breathe it. We could not live in it unless our space suits were pressurized. It would not protect us from meteors. It would not even carry sound.

The moon lacks something else essential to life. This is water. We will find no oceans, no lakes, no streams. If the moon ever had water, it has long since disappeared. Without an atmosphere, water would turn to vapor. It would float away into space, since the moon's gravity is much too weak to hold such vapor captive.

With no atmosphere and no water, the moon has no weather. Clouds never fill its sky. Rain and snow never moisten its surface. But the moon does have a climate—a terrible one of extreme heat and extreme cold.

The moon's day is about 28 earth days long—the time the moon takes to spin once on its axis. So periods of daylight and darkness each last two weeks. One side of the moon bakes in the sun for 14 days while the other freezes in darkness. The heat is very hot and the cold is very cold because there is no atmosphere to moderate them.

The same lack of atmosphere makes it hard to measure temperatures on the moon. On the earth, we measure the temperature of the air. On the moon, only the surface temperatures of solid objects can be measured. These vary greatly, depending on the color of the object, the material it's made of, and the angle at which sunlight hits it.

A flat black rock in full sunlight is much hotter than a light-colored rock; the dark color absorbs sunlight, while the light tends to reflect it. The side of a cliff is cooler than either because it receives only slanting sunlight. So the moon's surface has no one temperature by day. However, rocks exposed to direct sunlight reach temperatures higher than that of boiling water—which is 212 degrees Fahrenheit (212° F.)

Once the sun sets, the darkened surface of the moon cools quickly. Temperatures drop far below zero. By the end of the two-week night they may be as low as minus 250 degrees, giving the moon a temperature range of nearly 500 degrees.

Extremes of temperature are found even on the daylight side of the moon. The reason is that there is no air to spread heat. Step from sunlight into shadow, and you have stepped from a daylight temperature into the cold of night.

A harsh climate but no air, no water, no weather—these few facts explain much about the moon's appearance.

The moon's landscape is marked by the jagged, sharp lines of gaunt mountains, great craters, and deep cracks that have

Earth's Moon

mean diameter	2,160 miles
mean distance from Earth	238,857 miles
period of revolution	27⅓ earth days
period of rotation	27⅓ earth days
gravity	0.17 of earth's

probably looked the same for millions or billions of years. On this rugged land there is no rain to wear down rocks, no wind to shape them with driving sand, no frost to pry off slivers. On earth the jagged and the sharp have been smoothed, rounded, and worn down. On the moon only one such force shapes the landscape. This is the range of temperature. Expanding and contracting in the great heat and the great cold, rock formations may have been wrenched apart.

Mapping the face of the moon, astronomers have found ten lofty mountain ranges and many single peaks reaching thousands of feet above the surface. They have also noted some thirty plains. Dark gray in color and shaped like rough circles, the plains are the largest features we see on the moon. Together, they cover almost half of the moon's visible surface. To early astronomers, the dark plains looked like bodies of water. That is why the Latin names they were given all start with *mare,* meaning "sea."

Then there are several hundred great clefts in the surface of the moon. Through the telescope they look like crooked cracks, many of them a mile deep and 90 miles long. They may have been caused by "moonquakes" or some similar movement of rocks.

The most eye-catching features of the moon are its ring-shaped craters. Giant ones are between 60 and 140 miles in diameter—far bigger than any craters known on earth. Astronomers have counted more than 30,000 craters, ranging in diameter from 10 to 140 miles. In addition, the moon's surface is pockmarked with tiny craters too numerous to count.

Reaching out from some of the craters are brilliant streaks, called rays. Some, like those of the crater Tycho, extend for hundreds of miles. Astronomers are not sure what these rays are. They cannot be cracks or ridges because they cast no shadows. They are probably dust-fine material blown from the craters when these were formed.

At one time scientists believed that the craters were formed by volcanoes when the moon was young. Today most astronomers think that the craters formed when meteors struck the moon.

Millions or billions of years ago when the moon and earth were young, the solar system was full of wandering chunks of rocks, these scientists say. The rocks, some of which were the size of mountains, bombarded both the moon and the earth.

Meteors travel at tremendous speeds: some that hit the earth are traveling at 30 miles a second, which is 108,000 miles an hour. Such speed gives them energy equal to 250 times their own weight in dynamite. When a meteor hits, it is brought to a sudden stop. The stop releases the meteor's energy largely in the form of heat.

That, scientists think, is what happened on the moon. Mountain-sized meteors whipping through space slammed into the moon. Their energy was released as heat so great that it turned the meteor and the surrounding rock into gas. The temperature of the gas reached several million degrees, which means that it had enormous pressure. Like an exploding bomb, it expanded and (silently) blew a giant crater.

On the earth we see few signs of these ancient explosions. Scientists think the crater scars have been smoothed by erosion or hidden by plant life. They also think that after a time the bombardment of the earth stopped. Most of the giant meteors were gone. And they are the only ones that penetrate the earth's atmosphere. Smaller meteors burn up before they reach the earth's surface. Entering our atmosphere, they encounter friction. It changes their energy of motion into light and heat, which we see as a "falling star"—a sudden streak of light in the sky. Only their dust falls to earth.

The moon is different. Without an atmosphere, it has been struck by meteors of all sizes. Craters lie within craters. Craters overlap craters, forming a lacy pattern. On the moon's airless surface, no erosion takes place. So the craters remain, scars of violent explosions.

If the meteor theory is true, then the mountains ringing the craters may be gigantic heaps of loose rubble instead of solid masses. Low places between the mountains may be filled with dust finer than any we know on earth. The same fine dust may cover the plains in deep layers. Without rain to turn it into soil or clay, the dust would be as fresh and soft as when it fell. For the unwary explorer who blundered into it, the dust would be more treacherous than quicksand.

However, before the first men land on the moon, we shall know much more about it. Instrument-bearing rockets are already filling in large gaps in our knowledge. For example, until October 1959 no man had ever seen the far side of the moon.

Long ago, the moon's rotation slowed down to 27⅓ earth days, which is also the time required for the moon to circle our planet. For this reason, the moon always shows us the same face. Imaginative people made up exciting stories about what might be on the hidden side of the moon. But scientists said there was no reason to think the far side very different from the side we saw. In the fall of 1959 they were proved right. The Russian moon rocket Lunik III passed behind the moon and photographed its far side.

These first, fuzzy photographs showed the same kinds of mountains, plains, and craters that mark the moon's face. There was just one big difference between the two sides of the moon. The far side appeared to be much smoother than the side that faces Earth. Very few craters and plains showed up in the photographs.

Perhaps, some scientists said, the near side of the moon was more heavily bombarded by meteors. Other scientists suggested a different explanation. They believe the tug of Earth's gravity has affected the near side of the moon. Some surface markings may have been caused by the stresses and strains of this pull.

An earlier Russian moon rocket, Lunik II, scored a direct hit on the moon. Before crashing, it sent back two important pieces of information. Scientists say these clues probably mean that, unlike Earth, the moon is cold and solid at its center.

No one knows for sure what is at the center of the earth. But most scientists think the center is molten iron. They believe that movement of the molten iron is responsible for Earth's magnetic field. That is, it makes Earth act like a giant magnet.

No one has ever seen all the features of the moon at the same time. In fact, when the moon is full, its mountains cannot be clearly seen; there are no shadows visible to create relief against which the mountains can be seen.

Astronomers have mapped the face of the moon by watching it over a period of time, as it waxes from new to full and wanes from full to old. In the moon's long morning (the moon takes 27⅓ earth days to rotate once), its face is lighted from the side. The line of sunrise moves steadily across its face. Mountains climb out of the night as their peaks catch the first rays of sunlight. By noon the moon is full and the mountains are difficult to see. As the sun begins to set in the moon's afternoon, the moon is again lighted from the side and its mountains cast black shadows. At this time they can also be seen from Earth.

Earth's magnetic field traps cosmic rays from space. The rays form two belts of radiation around the earth, as United States scientists discovered.

Information from Lunik II seems to show that the moon has no magnetic field. Nor is it surrounded by belts of radiation. For these reasons, scientists think it must have a cold, solid center.

Rocket probes will continue for some time to come, each designed to give us certain kinds of information. For instance, United States scientists are planning to send a seismograph to the moon. If there are moonquakes or other movements of rock, they will register on the seismograph. The information will be radioed back to earth. From it scientists expect to learn what kind of rock makes up the main body of the moon; whether any of it is molten; whether moonquakes (if there are any) are like earthquakes; and what the dust and rubble are like. Not long ago, a Russian scientist reported seeing a volcano erupt on the moon, something no other modern scientist has ever observed. If there is volcanic action, it, too, will register.

Unmanned instruments may provide some idea of the mineral resources on the moon. If they don't, then this will be the first job assigned to explorers. The mineral resources will determine what use can be made of the moon.

Are there sources of water and oxygen? Are there materials from which food can be obtained? The answers to these questions must be yes, if we are going to establish a permanent base or colony on the moon. It is impossible to send to the moon everything that settlers might need. To a large extent, they must be self-supporting. And if the moon is to be a taking-off point for space trips, we must also discover sources of fuel.

Even though the moon is airless, waterless, and barren, these aims are not as impossible as they may sound.

Scientists expect to find on the moon many of the minerals known on earth. For they are sure that the birth of the moon was closely connected with the birth of the earth. Some scientists think the moon was torn out of the earth—from the basin of the Pacific Ocean. Others think the moon formed out of the same eddy of dust as the earth. In either case, the moon's minerals would be like ours.

On the earth, a large amount of oxygen is locked in the rocks that form our planet's crust. Water is also locked in the crust. Probably the same is true of the moon. Given enough power, moon explorers should be able to release and use the oxygen and water. For power, they would convert sunlight into electricity. In fact, one large company is already working on a model power plant for the moon.

Given water and oxygen, moon settlers could produce food. Plants, for example, can be grown without soil in water. An aviation company is experimenting with a greenhouse designed for the moon, growing plants in water, under low pressure, and in two-week periods of sunlight. Food can also be made by chemical means.

Apart from surveying the moon's 12 million square miles for mineral resources, explorers will have many other tasks. For one thing, we'll want an observatory on the moon. From it astronomers will be able to study the planets and stars as never before. The moon spins much more slowly than the earth, and it has no atmosphere to blur man's vision.

To all explorers, astronomers or not, many strange and wondrous things will be visible in the sky.

The moon is a world without dawn or dusk or blue sky, for there is no atmosphere to scatter the sun's light. Just before day, the black sky is still full of very bright stars. Then the sun begins to rise. Its faintly glowing corona appears above the horizon, followed by great arching flames of gas. Finally the sun itself appears, climbing (to our eyes) very, very slowly. It is colder looking and bluer than the sun as we see it from the earth.

Sun, flames, and corona move across the sky—and the sky is black. Step into the shadows, shield your eyes, and you will see the stars. Without the dimming effect of an atmosphere, they are very bright. Step back into the dazzling sunlight, and the stars vanish from the black sky. At sunset, 14 earth days later, the process is reversed. First the sun disappears, then the flames, then the corona. Night, 14 earth days long, falls upon that part of the moon.

Perhaps the most spectacular sight to be seen from the moon is Earth. Hanging in the moon's sky, it goes through phases from crescent to "full Earth" and back to crescent. It looks 14 times bigger in the moon's sky than the moon looks in ours, and it sheds a brighter light. The polar icecaps gleam, the continents stand out from behind patches of clouds. During a year the seasons change, bringing brown, white, and green to dif-

From the moon, you would see Earth with a halo of atmosphere.

ferent parts of the earth's surface. The earth is ringed by a shining halo—its atmosphere.

Look away from the sky, and there is the moon itself—a wild landscape of ragged mountains and giant craters. Etched in black and white, it is harsh and sharp, grim and savage. Airless, waterless, and possibly covered with treacherous dust, it is a hostile world for man. Yet the moon seems like a very pleasant place indeed when you compare it with its first cousin, Mercury.

Mercury (foreground) is a bare ball.
Venus (background) is wrapped in
clouds.

5

Mercury and Venus

Earth   Venus   Mercury

Between the earth and the sun lie two planets, Mercury and Venus. Since they are neighbors, you might expect them to be somewhat alike. Yet they are very different. One is nothing but a bare ball of rock and metal. The other is wrapped in clouds so thick that no one has ever seen through them.

Mercury is the bare ball. Scarcely bigger than our moon, it is the smallest planet in the solar system. As the innermost planet, it is also the fastest moving. That is why it is named after fleet-footed Mercury, the messenger of the gods.

Traveling the long ellipse of its orbit, Mercury takes only 88 earth days to complete one trip around the sun. A person who has lived 15 earth years would be 62 on Mercury. Or, if he chose, he could claim to be only 62 *days* old. For Mercury also takes 88 earth days to complete one spin on its axis.

Astronomers think that Mercury used to spin much faster. But, they say, ages ago the gravitational pull of the sun slowed the spinning of the small planet until its day became as long as its year. Now Mercury always keeps the same face toward the sun, just as the moon always keeps the same face toward the earth.

As a result, the side of Mercury facing the sun is a land of ever-day while the other side knows only unending night. At a mean distance of 36 million miles from the sun, the day side is forever exposed to blazing heat. The temperature there is probably more than 700 degrees Fahrenheit—so hot that lead and tin would melt. The day side is separated from the night side by two twilight zones, where the sun bobs up and down on the horizon. Beyond these is the side that never sees the sun. Its only light comes from the stars and planets. Its only heat—if there is any—is a trickle reaching it through the ground. Here the temperature must be about minus 450 degrees, only a few degrees above absolute zero.

If Mercury had an atmosphere, some heat would be carried around to that cold dark land. But Mercury has little or no air. No real atmosphere could exist under Mercurian conditions.

In the same long-ago past when the planet's spinning slowed, Mercury probably had an atmosphere—and lost it. The intense heat of the sun speeded up the movement of the gas molecules in the atmosphere. And Mercury's surface gravity was too weak to hold that envelope of air. The gases escaped into space, leaving Mercury as airless as the moon.

In the ages that followed, the fierce heat of the sun baked

Mercury's surface dry. The day side must now be a parched land where eternal sunlight blazes on rocks and everything looks white in the intense glare. The landscape must be as rugged and jagged and bleak as the moon's. There must be huge craters formed by meteors, gaunt mountains, and gigantic fissures in the ground, cracked open by extremes of temperature.

But to describe Mercury is to guess. No one has ever had a really good look at the innermost planet. Astronomers studying its surface can make out only "light areas" and "dark areas."

Mercury

Figures used in this book are based on those in the 7th edition of *Astronomy* by Robert H. Baker (1959).

mean diameter	2,900 miles
mean distance from sun	35,960,000 miles
mean speed of revolution	107,900 miles per hour
length of year	88 earth days
length of day	88 earth days
gravity	0.26 of earth's
temperature range	700° F. to —450° F.
transits	1960, 1970, 1973, 1986, 1993, 1999
moons	none

They see no details. Descriptions of Mercury are based on what they think must have happened under the conditions they know exist.

Mercury is difficult to study because it is a small planet that lies between us and the sun. Most of the time it is hidden by the sun's glare. It never crosses our night sky, but appears only for short periods just after sunset and just before sunrise. It can be seen only if the sky is very clear.

Because it lies inside the earth's orbit, we see Mercury go through phases. The phases are like the moon's except for one thing. We never see a "full" Mercury. When the full face is turned toward the earth, the sun's glare hides the planet from view.

We also see Mercury crossing the sun. Every few years, Mercury appears to edge onto the left side of the sun's disk, taking shape as a small black dot. If the planet blocked more of the sun from view, this would be counted an eclipse. As it is, we say the planet is in transit.

If Mercury had an atmosphere, it would shine as a halo each time the planet was in transit. The lack of a halo means that Mercury is airless. Airless, it is waterless. Airless and waterless, it is lifeless—a bare ball of rock and metal.

Venus is one of the loveliest and most tantalizing planets. It is closer to us than any other planet—sometimes swinging within 26 million miles of the earth. It is at times brighter than any other planet or star in our sky. Yet we know very little about it. Venus is cloaked in a thick atmosphere of dense

When Mercury moves between
the sun and the Earth, we can
see it as a black dot crossing the
face of the sun. This is called a
transit of Mercury.

SUN

MERCURY

EARTH

yellow-white clouds. No one has ever seen the planet's surface.

This is particularly tantalizing because in several ways Venus is suitable for supporting life. It is about the right distance from the sun. And it is an Earth-sized planet—just a little smaller and a little lighter in weight than the earth. Its gravity holds captive an atmosphere about the size of our own.

That atmosphere is all we see of Venus. We can probe it with radio waves, but we cannot see through it. The solid body of the planet remains invisible to us, shielded by gleaming clouds.

The clouds make Venus so bright that you can see it in broad daylight if you know where and when to look. The same brightness has made it one of the most familiar planets even though, like Mercury, it appears in the night sky for only short periods after sunset and before sunrise.

To the ancients, who named lovely Venus after the goddess of love, such behavior was puzzling. It was not really understood until the time of Galileo. Then astronomers finally learned that the planets circled the sun and that the orbit of Venus lay between the earth and sun.

With the invention of the telescope, many astronomers began to study Venus closely. They assumed that what they saw was the surface of the planet and they began to make drawings of it. Around 1730 an Italian astronomer produced a map showing oceans, continents, and other features that resembled the earth's. A number of other astronomers also reported surface markings on Venus.

Today there is every reason to believe that those astronomers were mistaken in what they saw. Venus's dense clouds are hundreds of miles deep. And it is most unlikely that anyone ever saw the planet's surface. Probably earlier astronomers were seeing the markings that appear in Venus's atmosphere.

Modern telescopes show light and dark patches that appear and disappear. They may last for a few days or they may vanish in a matter of hours. Probably they are caused by the thickening or thinning of clouds torn by raging winds below.

Certain other strange markings also appear on Venus from time to time. When Venus is in its crescent phase, two bright patches are often seen at the tips of the horns. No one knows what these are.

Then at times a strange pale light shines on the dark (or night) side of Venus. Astronomers call it ashen light, but they are not sure of what it is. Some think it may be earthshine—a dim reflection of light from the earth. Others think it may be akin to the auroras seen in the earth's sky. Earthly auroras are caused by electrified particles that make the atmosphere glow. It is quite possible that something similar takes place in the atmosphere of Venus.

All markings on Venus are faint and fleeting. Most of the time there are none to be seen at all. There is only the gleaming blanket of clouds that hides the surface from our eyes.

As a result, most of what is known about Venus is based on what scientists can tell from the clouds.

No one can observe how long Venus takes to rotate on its axis. Since the surface can't be seen, there is no way astronomers can time the rotation of a fixed feature like a mountain.

But by studying the clouds they have come to think that Venus rotates slowly. One day on Venus perhaps equals between 20 and 30 earth days.

Astronomers reason this way. Suppose Venus rotated as fast as the earth. At that rate the atmosphere would take on the shape of a slightly flattened ball. Since there are no signs of flattening, Venus cannot be rotating nearly as fast as the earth. Or suppose Venus did not rotate at all. In that case, its clouds would condense on the night side, which is colder. Since that does not happen, Venus must be rotating.

Venus

mean diameter	7,600 miles
mean distance from sun	67,200,000 miles
mean speed of revolution	79,000 miles per hour
length of year	225 earth days
length of day	20 to 30 earth days ?
gravity	0.85 of earth's
temperature	
outer atmosphere	130° F. to −10° F.
60-100 miles above surface	30° F.
surface	585° F.
transits	1874, 1882, 2004, 2012
moons	none

Then, too, astronomers have measured the heat given off by the surface of the clouds. The sunny side of the atmosphere is 130 degrees Fahrenheit, while the night side is minus 10 degrees. If the night side were a region of ever-dark, its temperature would be much lower.

By such means, astronomers have concluded that Venus is a slowly rotating planet.

A number of years ago astronomers also began to study Venus's atmosphere with the spectroscope. And the spectroscope showed that the clouds contain large amounts of carbon dioxide.

People who didn't know much about science decided this fact could mean only one thing: Venus must be covered with giant plants thriving in steamy swamps. For, they said, everyone knows that carbon dioxide is what plants need.

Actually, the carbon dioxide was almost certain proof that no such plants existed on Venus. It is perfectly true that the earth's plants require carbon dioxide—but they replace it with oxygen. If such plants existed on Venus, they would have changed its atmosphere just as plants changed ours.

And the spectroscope showed no free oxygen in the atmosphere of Venus. It might, scientists said, exist there in such small amounts that it did not show up in the spectroscope. But there could not be large amounts of it. Being a light gas, oxygen would tend to float to the top of Venus's atmosphere, above the heavier gas of carbon dioxide. There the spectroscope would have found it.

The spectroscope did not show water in Venus's clouds either. But no one was sure of the reason. Perhaps there simply wasn't any water in the clouds. Or perhaps it was impossible to detect because of all the water in Earth's own atmosphere.

Some scientists felt sure that Venus's clouds consisted of drops of water. If this was so, then Venus might have a great deal of water at lower altitudes. The surface of the planet might be a vast ocean.

Other scientists were convinced that no water existed on Venus. The clouds, they said, were really masses of very fine dust blown up from a desert-like surface by tornado-strong winds.

Still a third theory held that the clouds were a smog of fine oil drops and that Venus was covered with an ocean of oil.

On other matters, scientists were in closer agreement. For one thing, they all thought Venus must be very hot.

Venus is closer to the sun than the earth is. And its carbon-dioxide atmosphere must trap the sun's heat. Heat from the sun penetrates the atmosphere in short-wave radiation. The planet's surface absorbs the heat and then gives it off in long waves. Most of the long waves are blocked by the carbon dioxide and trapped on Venus. So Venus must be rather like a greenhouse, where short waves pass through the glass and long waves are trapped inside.

Venus is also probably pitch dark, for its clouds are so thick that little or no sunlight can penetrate them. Possibly the only light that brightens the surface of Venus comes from great bolts of lightning or from erupting volcanoes.

None of this was very encouraging to those who hoped to find life on Venus. Still, the possibility could not be ruled out.

Venus might have polar regions cool enough to support life. As for oxygen and light, their lack would not rule out life either. Earth itself has many tiny organisms that live without them.

Some scientists made still another suggestion. Perhaps, they said, life was about to begin on Venus. Beneath the stormy clouds, the first simple forms of life might be about to develop. A carbon-dioxide atmosphere is typical of a world in a very early stage of development.

Now two new pieces of evidence raise many questions about all these theories.

The first is proof of water vapor in Venus's atmosphere. It was brought back by two daring scientists who ballooned 80,000 feet up into Earth's atmosphere. At that height the balloon was above 98 per cent of the water in our air. And this time the spectroscope showed that there was definitely some water vapor in Venus's cloudy atmosphere.

The discovery raised high hopes of finding life on Venus. For life as we know it must have water.

But the second piece of evidence is very discouraging. It seems to show that life on Venus is impossible. The planet is too hot—much hotter than anyone ever guessed. The surface of Venus is a broiling 585 degrees, day and night.

The figure comes from a three-year study of Venus by radio

telescope. Radio telescopes were used to pick up radio waves given off by Venus. (Radio waves from a heated body are an indication of its temperature.) When the radio waves from Venus were analyzed, they showed an average temperature of 585 degrees.

Another and different study confirms the figure. In July 1959, Venus eclipsed the bright star Regulus. Astronomers seized the chance to measure the dimming of Regulus' light as it penetrated the atmosphere of Venus. From this they learned that 60 to 100 miles above the planet's surface the temperature averages 30 degrees. On the surface the temperature is close to 600 degrees.

At such temperatures, no water could possibly exist on the surface of Venus. If there are seas, they must be of molten metal.

We know no form of life that can exist without water. And we know none that could live at temperatures close to 600 degrees.

The best guess today is that Venus is chiefly a vast and sandy desert. The desert is flat, for wind-driven sand has long ago worn down the hills and filled in the hollows. It is dark, for sunlight does not penetrate the clouds. It is dry, for rain cannot fall on it. And it is lifeless.

Before long, much more will be known about Venus. Powerful radar and other instruments will probe the clouds, mapping the surface and timing the rotation. Satellites and rockets will relay back information on what the clouds are made of. Someday valiant explorers may descend through the clouds.

But that day will not come for a long time. The first planet men will visit is almost certain to be Mars. Mars is our other close neighbor and the only other planet in our solar system that may support life.

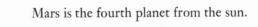

Mars is the fourth planet from the sun.

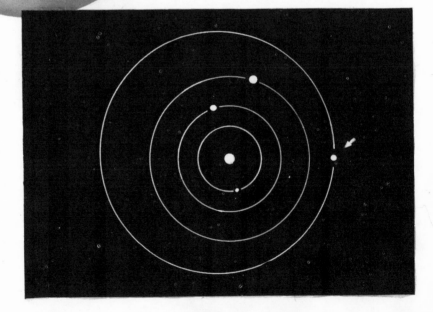

6

Mars, the Red Planet

Mars

Earth

Of all the planets in our solar system, Mars is most like Earth.

It is a small, solid planet, whose diameter is a little more than half of the earth's. Among the inner planets, only Mars and Earth have moons. Mars has two tiny ones. Since its axis is tilted like ours, Mars has seasons—spring, summer, fall, and winter. Being farther from the sun, Mars travels a longer orbit at speeds slower than the earth's. As a result, its year is almost twice as long as ours; its seasons are longer; and its climate is colder. But a day on Mars is only a little longer than a day on earth. And Mars is the only other planet with an atmosphere much like ours.

Finally, there are signs that life may exist on Mars. That is what makes Mars the most exciting planet. It also makes Mars the most controversial. For more than eighty years, scientists have been arguing over the question of life on Mars.

If you could look at Mars through a big telescope, you would find it rather disappointing. You would see only a rather fuzzy, reddish ball marked with vague dark patches. Depending on when you looked at Mars, you might also see a white patch at the pole tilted toward you. But you would see nothing that was likely to stir up an argument, for you would see no details. It takes the practiced eye of an astronomer to see Mars fairly clearly.

Viewed without a telescope in the night sky, Mars has a reddish hue. In ancient times, this color won Mars its name. The color reminded people of blood, and so the planet was named for the god of war.

The telescope shows that Mars looks red because it is red. Most of its surface is covered with reddish regions that range in tone from deep red to yellowish white.

The red regions never change from season to season or year to year. But from time to time a yellow veil spreads over them —in the way that sandstorms sweep certain parts of earth. For these reasons, astronomers think that the red regions must be sandy deserts. Their color may come from rusting iron oxide, like the red in Arizona's Painted Desert.

The deserts seem to be fairly flat. If they had mountains, the peaks would climb into view at the line between day and night, just as they do on the moon. But no such thing happens. Some astronomers think that Mars did once have mountains but that they were worn down by raging sandstorms. Perhaps hills and plateaus remain. If so, the shadows they cast are too small to be seen.

The brilliant white icecaps stand out more clearly than any other feature of Mars, and they are very interesting. Here there is movement and change. In regular rhythm the icecaps advance and retreat with the seasons.

By winter's end an icecap may cover some four million square miles. With the coming of spring, it begins to shrink. It changes at first slowly, then with increasing speed. By mid-spring, dark cracks appear in the cap. The ice splits into big sections; the big sections split into small ones. The pieces vanish, but part of the cap remains. Even in mid-summer the cap is still a dazzling white spot at the pole.

Near the end of summer, patches of white cloud appear in the polar region. By fall they have curtained the entire area. When the veil of clouds breaks up in late winter, the icecap has re-formed.

In some years, the icecaps are bigger than in other years. But the general pattern is always the same. Even the dark cracks appear in the same places every year. Probably the ice is running into obstacles—like hills or low mountains—and tearing apart.

The Martian icecaps are not thick fields of ice and snow, like the earth's. They seem to be just a thin covering of frost, perhaps a few inches thick. They evaporate in the warmth of the spring and summer sun. They condense under the cloud cover of winter.

These thin caps of ice are the only water known to exist on Mars. Melt them and they might just about fill Lake Erie. In a way, that doesn't seem like enough water to make much difference. Yet when the icecaps start to melt, a second very interesting change occurs. This change takes place in the dark patches that cover a fifth of Mars's surface.

Astronomers cannot be sure what the dark patches are. But they watch with fascination the changes that come over them. When a polar icecap melts, a wave of color washes over the dark areas in that hemisphere. Along with the color change come changes in shape and size.

The changes begin near the edge of the melting polar cap and move toward the equator. It is almost certain that the changes are caused by the melting. But no one knows whether the melting ice runs toward the equator as surface water. Possibly it moves above the surface, traveling to the other pole in the form of water vapor.

What are the dark patches? Are they regions of plant life that waken under the magic touch of water? Or are they something else?

Modern scientific arguments about life on Mars hinge on those questions. But the argument itself goes back more than eighty years to the famous study of Mars made by Giovanni Schiaparelli, the Italian astronomer.

Schiaparelli's study began in 1877. That year Mars was in an excellent position for observation. It was close to the earth and fully lighted by the sun. Schiaparelli himself was a fine astronomer with a very good telescope. Everything, then, was just right. It resulted in the first detailed description of Mars and the start of a great argument.

Like other astronomers of his time, Schiaparelli thought that

In 1877 an American astronomer named Asaph Hall discovered that Mars has two tiny moons. He named them Deimos (which means "horror") and Phobos ("fear") after the two companions of Mars, the Roman god of war.

Deimos is so small, only 5 or 10 miles in diameter, that from Mars it would appear as a pinpoint of light. Phobos is twice as big and more than twice as close to Mars. Seen from Mars, it would be about a quarter the size of the moon we see from Earth.

Someday these tiny moons may be landing places for space ships from the earth. Their gravity is so weak that a space ship could land or take off with almost no power. In fact, a man could probably jump right off Deimos, reaching escape velocity with his muscles alone.

the dark areas were seas and the reddish areas continents. But he found a great range of colors in both. He noted certain areas that were sometimes yellow and sometimes brown or black like the "seas." These, he thought, must be swamps.

Searching out more and more detail, Schiaparelli noted a number of dark streaks on the face of Mars. They appeared to be thin dark lines which crossed the "continents" and linked the "seas." Schiaparelli called the lines *canali*, the Italian word for "channels."

The longer he studied Mars, the more *canali* he found. Mapping them, he discovered that they formed a network, lacing the planet and crisscrossing one another. And in many ways they were rather curious:

(1) The lines ran straight and true. They did not look at all like the rivers of earth, which curve and meander and sometimes twist back on themselves. However, they did always seem to link the dark areas. And where they crossed one another there was usually a small dark patch. Schiaparelli thought these dark spots were lakes.

(2) The lines varied greatly in size. Some *canali* were short and narrow, perhaps 200 miles long and 50 miles wide. Some ran straight across Mars for a thousand miles or more and were 100 to 200 miles wide. Short or long, each had a definite beginning and a definite end.

(3) Sometimes *canali* disappeared. The change might take place in a week or it might take a year. But it always happened in the same way. The color of a line would grow gradually lighter until it blended with the surrounding land and the line

vanished. The reverse also happened. *Canali* might suddenly appear where none had been before. Schiaparelli explained the changes this way. The *canali*, he said, are deep furrows in the land. In spring and summer polar ice melts and water flows into the furrows. This gives them their dark color. Then, as the water soaks into the ground and also evaporates, the furrows dry up and vanish.

(4) Certain *canali* doubled. This change usually took place in the months just before or after the melting of a polar icecap. *Canali* that had been single lines would double in the course of a few days or a few hours. Where there had been just one line, a second would appear. It was parallel to the first, running beside it so that the two looked like railroad tracks. The distance between the two lines might range from 30 miles to 400 miles.

Schiaparelli was not the first man to see dark lines on Mars. But nobody else had studied them so long and carefully. Nobody else had found so many. Nobody else had mapped them. And nobody else had given them a name. Schiaparelli's name for the lines meant "channels." But as his work was translated into English people did not use that word. Instead they used "canals," perhaps because that English word was so like the Italian *canali*.

The change was an important one. A channel can be a natural waterway or a man-made one. A canal is always man-made. The very use of the word "canals" implied that intelligent beings had built them.

Then there was the nature of the canals. They ran absolutely straight and true. They appeared to be part of a plan. Surely, people said, the canals could not have occurred naturally. They must have been built—and for a purpose. If this was so, then intelligent life must exist on Mars or must have existed there in the past.

The canals touched off a storm of argument about life on Mars. Some people said the canals were proof of life on Mars. Others claimed life on Mars was impossible. Schiaparelli himself never took a stand on this matter. He did not think the *canali* were proof of life; neither did he think life on Mars was impossible.

The argument became even more heated as other astronomers turned their telescopes on Mars. Some claimed to have seen just what Schiaparelli did. Some failed to see any canals at all. And that raised the question of whether the canals really existed.

Among the astronomers who reported seeing canals was an American, Percival Lowell. Like Schiaparelli, Lowell had made Mars his special study. In 1894 he set up an observatory at Flagstaff, Arizona, to study the planets, particularly Mars.

One of the first discoveries made by Lowell concerned the dark areas or "seas." Working in the clear, dry air of Arizona, he observed the "seas" in far greater detail than anyone before him. And what he saw convinced him that they could not be large bodies of water.

For one thing, the dark areas, like the reddish ones, were crossed by canals. Further, the dark areas changed both their color and their shape from season to season.

Soon after an icecap started to melt, canals appeared in the polar regions. The darkening of canals spread toward the equator and beyond it at a rate of about 50 miles a day. At the same time, the dark areas changed their shapes. And during the wet season their color changed from a dusky shade to green and later to brown and yellow.

The dark areas might be marshes. But Lowell believed that the change of color was actually much more meaningful. He believed that the dark patches consisted of plant life that responded to the seasons just as our plant life does.

Year after year Lowell studied the canals, the dark areas, the changes that took place on the face of Mars. As he did so, an idea began to take shape in his mind, an idea that gave meaning to the canals and told a tragic story. This was Lowell's famous theory about Mars, which he announced in 1906. Lowell believed that Mars had once supported a great civilization; then a drastic change turned Mars into a dying planet where life was slowly but surely being snuffed out.

This is the way Lowell reasoned:

If we could sit on Venus and look at the earth, every six months we would see a strange and beautiful change taking place. In spring half of the earth would start to waken from its winter's sleep. White and browns would vanish. In their place would come a spreading light green that moved slowly toward the pole and at the same time became darker.

On Mars, Lowell pointed out, something very similar happens. In spring we see a wave of changing color spread across half the planet. But there is one important difference. On the earth, green starts near the equator and moves toward the pole. On Mars the wave of color starts near the pole and moves toward the equator. The reason for the difference is water.

On the earth, water is always available (except in deserts). Plants, then, are called to life by the sun and by the sun alone. But Mars, Lowell said, is different. Its plant life finds no water in the soil. So it is doubly dependent on the sun. It needs the warmth of the sun, just as the earth's plants do. But it cannot grow until the sun has melted the icecap and unlocked the water supply. For this reason, Martian plants first show signs of new life near the pole. That is where water first becomes available. As the water spreads toward the equator, plants along the way begin their spring growth.

Next, Lowell took up the question of intelligent life on Mars. It is easy, he pointed out, to see the spread and growth of plants on another planet. By their presence they change the color and shape of whole regions. But we would not see similar signs of animal life. In fact, we would recognize animal life "not by its body, but by its mind," Lowell wrote. "Across the gulf of space it could be recognized only by the imprint it had made on the face of Mars."

The imprint, he said, was the canals—the long straight lines that only intelligent beings might have made. As he had seen and drawn them, the canals were clearly artificial and made for a purpose.

Their purpose, said Lowell, was to carry water across the dry planet and irrigate the fertile regions where the Martians lived.

How could they carry water *all* over Mars when water runs only downhill? Lowell supposed that the Martians must have built a vast pumping system to move water through the canals. The power required, he calculated, would be 4,000 times the power of Niagara Falls. Such a power system was a great engineering achievement. It could have been built only by beings who were highly intelligent—and desperate.

The Martians, according to Lowell, had good reason to be desperate. They had to build canals and pumping stations because the water supply was failing. Slowly, over a long period of time, Mars had become drier and drier. To supply their needs, the Martians reached out to what sources of water remained. They built canals and pumped water to places where

Mars

mean diameter	4,200 miles
mean distance from sun	141,600,000 miles
mean speed of revolution	54,200 miles per hour
length of year	687 earth days
length of day	24½ earth hours
gravity	0.38 of earth's
temperature range	70° F. to −150° F.
moons	2

it was needed, much as we pipe water to big cities. As the planet grew still drier, its surface was laced with canals. Finally the Martians had to tap their one last source of water—the distant icecaps. Their very lives depended on the yearly melting of the icecaps. For this reason their whole way of life centered around the canals and pumping stations.

At best, Lowell said, the Martians were simply buying time. There was no way in which they could halt the drying up of their planet, no way in which they could preserve their scanty supply of water. One day the water would be gone.

At the end of his book, *Mars as the Abode of Life*, Lowell said of Mars: "The process that brought it to its present pass must go on to the bitter end, until the last spark of Martian life goes out. The drying up of the planet is certain to proceed until its surface can support no life at all. Slowly but surely time will snuff it out. When the last ember is thus extinguished, the planet will roll, a dead world, through space."

That, very briefly, is Lowell's account of life on Mars. As everyone agrees, it is a brilliant theory. But if you ask how close it comes to fact—that's where the argument begins.

If Mars is really laced with canals, then Lowell's theory may well be true. But if there are no canals, then the whole theory collapses. And most astronomers today say there are no canals on Mars.

If there are no canals, then what did Schiaparelli and Lowell see? Or, if there are canals, why don't today's astronomers see them? In fact, why don't all astronomers see the same thing when they look at Mars?

The answers to those questions lie in the problems of viewing Mars and recording what one has seen. For, while astronomers see Mars better than any other planet, their view of it is still far from ideal.

To begin with, any time we look out from Earth into the solar system, our view is blurred. We cannot see clearly through the earth's atmosphere. There is no way to bring Mars into strong, sharp focus.

Secondly, astronomers cannot observe Mars night after night and always get the same view, as they do with the moon. The distance between Earth and Mars varies greatly. For one thing, the shapes of their orbits are different. Mars orbits the sun in an ellipse. Earth's orbit is almost a circle. And, of course, the two planets move at different speeds. As a result, Earth passes Mars only once every twenty-six months.

When Earth does pass Mars, the two planets are said to be in opposition. At these times Mars, Earth, and the sun are lined up. Astronomers see the face of Mars fully lighted. Some oppositions are better than others. The two planets may be as much as 62 million miles apart. But once every fifteen years Mars is in opposition and only 35 million miles away.

All of this means that occasionally Mars can be seen much better than at other times.

A third problem has to do with recording what is seen. We can photograph Mars, but the results are never very clear. Since Mars shines by reflected light, it must be photographed with a time exposure. And movements of the earth's atmosphere blur the picture. The best records of Mars are made by observers who draw what they see. But it is almost impossible to draw in detail everything that the eye has seen at any one moment.

And this raises still a fourth problem—the observer himself. Some people see better than others. Some have more experience in observing through a telescope. Some draw better. To make matters worse, when a detail is faintly glimpsed it may look like one thing to one person and something completely different to another. Finally, our eyes do sometimes trick us. Look down the railroad, and your eyes tell you that the tracks meet in the distance. Turn a photo of the moon upside down, and what looked like a crater may suddenly turn into a mountain.

For all these reasons, observers report having seen Mars in different ways.

A number of astronomers, including some very great ones, claim to have seen canals on Mars. Perhaps they really did see them. Perhaps they saw better than other men. Perhaps they were more expert at picking out details. Perhaps Mars has changed—drying up more—since their time.

But most modern scientists say that there is no network of canals on Mars. They have seen only a few dark lines on Mars. Photos show only a few. And these lines, the astronomers say, mark natural formations.

The same astronomers make this point, too: our eyes have a tendency to link a series of vague, distant markings and see them as a straight line. You can test this yourself if you draw a row of dots an eighth of an inch apart on a sheet of paper. Ask a friend to hold up the paper thirty feet away. You will see not the dots but a straight line. In the same way, an able observer

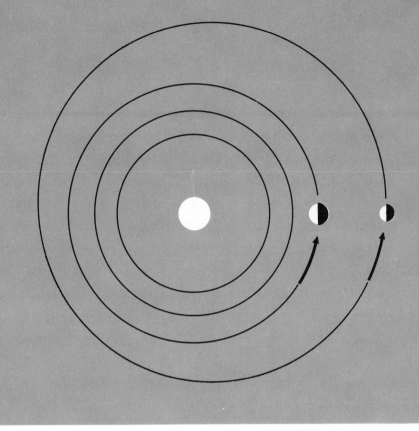

When Mars and Earth are in opposition, astronomers can see the face of Mars fully lighted.

staring at faint detail on Mars might "see" lines where there were none.

At best, then, the canals are doubtful. More probably they do not exist.

Without the canals, no sign of intelligent life can be seen on Mars. In fact, none could be. Even if great cities existed, they would not show up in a telescope.

Since the scientist cannot hope to see signs of intelligent life on Mars, he must go at the matter another way. First he asks: What conditions exist on Mars? Then he asks: Could these conditions support life? Is there a breathable atmosphere, water, and temperatures that are neither too hot nor too cold?

Scientists know that Mars has an atmosphere—but earth life would not be able to breathe in it. The one gas that definitely exists in Mars's atmosphere is carbon dioxide. Long and careful studies have turned up no sign of oxygen. If there is any, it must exist in tiny quantities. There may once have been a good deal of oxygen in Mars's atmosphere. If so, it vanished as it became fixed in the soil of the planet. That is, it was locked up in the deserts.

Besides carbon dioxide, the atmosphere probably contains large amounts of nitrogen, a gas that cannot be detected in the spectroscope. Nitrogen is a gas that could be held by the weak gravity of Mars. If they ever existed, light gases like hydrogen and helium long ago escaped into space.

Because of the weak gravity, air pressure on the surface of Mars is low and the air itself is thin—too low and too thin for most forms of life.

Temperatures on Mars vary greatly because the planet's distance from the sun varies greatly. When Mars is close to the sun, temperatures on a summer's day may rise to 70 or 80 degrees Fahrenheit. But during most Martian summers, temperatures are rarely above freezing. In the long polar night, the temperature may well drop to minus 150 degrees.

The only known water is released from the melting icecaps, and there is not very much of it. Some scientists have suggested that water may be hidden under the surface of Mars, as it is in many desert areas of the earth. If so, this water does not appear to be in use.

Mars, then, has little or no oxygen in its atmosphere. The planet is cold much of the time. And water is scarce.

Yet many scientists today feel sure that one kind of life does exist on Mars. The evidence for plant life—for simple, hardy plants—is very strong.

These scientists believe that the dark regions on Mars can be nothing except living plants. How else, they ask, can we explain the changes in these regions? What else could change the shape of the regions? What else could account for the colors that change with the seasons?

A few scientists have replied that the dark regions could be lifeless and still show change. They might, for example, consist of sand or minerals that change their color when wet.

That does not seem very likely, other scientists argue. If the dark areas were lifeless, then the yellow sandstorms of Mars should long since have hidden them from view. As it is, the dark areas renew themselves each year. Surely they must be hardy, vigorous plants. Surviving cold, drought, and sandstorms, they come back each spring to make a quick and sweeping color change on the face of Mars.

No one has yet proved that the dark patches are plants. Yet evidence keeps turning up in favor of this theory. To take one example: in 1956 Mars was in opposition and as close to the earth as it ever comes. In 1958 Mars was again in opposition and fairly close. In both those years, Dr. William M. Sinton of the

Lowell Observatory studied Mars with a spectroscope. He found evidence of molecules of living matter on Mars—what scientists call organic molecules. He said, "This evidence and the well-known seasonal changes of the dark areas make it extremely probable that vegetation in some form is present."

It's impossible to say what kind of plants may be growing on Mars, for we know only earth plants. Still, here on our planet, there are plants that grow in extreme cold and in extreme drought. More than 60 species of lichens have been found growing on the stony peaks of a mountain range in Antarctica. An expedition to the Sahara studied soils whose moisture content was less than 0.5 per cent; in the soil samples, scientists found 98 species of bacteria, 28 species of fungi, and 84 species of algae. Such evidence makes it likely that Martian plants—if they exist—are very much like our lichens, mosses, and algae.

Where there are plants, there may be animals. If there are animals on Mars, they would be more like bacteria than like rabbits. On the earth certain bacteria can live without oxygen; others can live without water. Possibly such "animals" live on Mars. Or Martian bacteria may live by attacking plants and using the oxygen in them. They may have learned to store water. Perhaps they are frozen every winter and thawed out every spring. On the earth, small organisms such as bacteria and protozoa can be frozen for years and thawed out alive and healthy.

On our own planet certain kinds of life survive under extreme conditions. There is no reason why this should not also be true of Mars. But life on Mars can hardly be more than very simple and primitive. So far as we know, no kind of intelligent life could possibly exist on Mars today.

It will take a space probe or even a landing on Mars before we know for sure if the red planet supports plant life. If it does, we may find that lichens and mosses are the only kind of life that ever had a foothold on Mars. Or we may find they are all that remain of many forms of life that once existed there.

The orbits of most of the asteroids lie between the orbits of Mars and Jupiter.

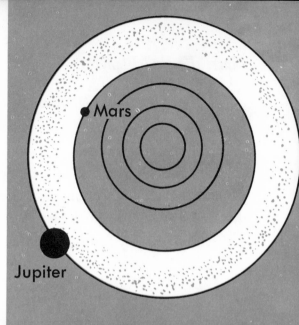

7

The Asteroids:
A Missing Planet?

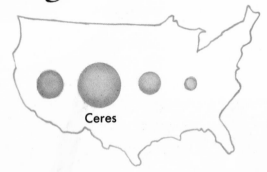

Ceres

A belt of space 340 million miles wide separates Mars from its outer neighbor, Jupiter. In that belt one of the strangest searches of modern astronomy took place some 160 years ago. It was a search for a missing planet. And it resulted in the discovery of hundreds of planets.

The story begins with a German astronomer named Johann Elert Bode. Like other astronomers, Bode knew that the distances separating the planets vary. Outward from the sun, these distances grow greater and greater. For example, there is a much bigger gap between the orbits of Jupiter and Saturn than between the orbits of Earth and Mars.

Studying these distances, Bode discovered a mathematical relationship among them. He developed a simple means of expressing it, which has come to be called Bode's Law.

The law is a quick and easy way of working out the relative distances of the planets from the sun. That is, it does not tell you how many miles a planet is from the sun. But it tells you that Mercury is less than half of Earth's distance from the sun, while Saturn is 10 times Earth's distance from the sun. (The table on the next page shows how Bode's Law works.)

Bode found that his table worked very neatly except for one thing—the gap between Mars and Jupiter. There was no known planet between these two. To make the figures fit the facts, Bode would have had to omit number 2.8 from his series.

The law was not a theory. It did not attempt to explain anything. It simply summed up certain known facts. Still, it seemed curious that the law should work in every case but one. So Bode began to wonder about that gap between Mars and Jupiter. Mightn't it be possible that there *was* a planet there, one that hadn't been discovered?

Other astronomers agreed that the gap was strange indeed. They began to search the sky, looking for an unknown planet. In fact, a group of German astronomers who called themselves Celestial Police set out to study every mile of space between Mars and Jupiter. But the first discovery was made by someone else on the night of January 1, 1801. An Italian astronomer named Giuseppi Piazzi found a small celestial body in the belt of space between Mars and Jupiter. According to Bode's Law a planet in the belt should be 2.8 times the distance of Earth from the sun. Piazzi's find, which was later named Ceres, had a relative distance of 2.77.

Ceres, however, had a diameter of only 480 miles. So astron-

Bode's Law

(for estimating relative distances of planets from the sun)

			sums	Bode's distance	true distance
Mercury	0	4	4	0.4	0.39
Venus	3	4	7	0.7	0.72
Earth	6	4	10	1.0	1.00
Mars	12	4	16	1.6	1.52
X	24	4	28	2.8	2.77
Jupiter	48	4	52	5.2	5.20
Saturn	96	4	100	10.0	9.54
Uranus	192	4	196	19.6	19.19
Neptune	384	4	388	38.8	30.07
Pluto	768	4	772	77.2	39.46

Not known in Bode's time

How Bode's Law works: Beside the names of the planets, you write a series of numbers—0, 3, 6, 12, 24, and so on. You find the next number by doubling the one before (except in the case of zero).

Next, you add 4 to each number.

Then you divide each sum by 10; that is, you insert a decimal point before the last figure of each number. The result is the estimated relative distance of each planet from the sun as compared with Earth's distance (1.0). Venus, for example, is 0.7 of Earth's distance from the sun.

The final column of figures gives you the true relative distance. As you can see, the true distances are very close to Bode's, except for Neptune and Pluto. Some astronomers believe that Pluto is not a true planet.

omers began to wonder if this was really the planet predicted
by Bode's Law. Thinking there might be something else in the
gap, they again turned their telescopes on it. Sure enough—
there *was* something else. A second little planet was discovered.
This one, Pallas, was even smaller than Ceres. Soon after, two
more were found—Juno and Vesta. Still others kept turning
up. By 1870 more than a hundred little planets had been found
between Mars and Jupiter. By 1890 three hundred were
known. Today two thousand have been catalogued, and astronomers suspect that the total number may be fifty thousand.
Ceres remains the largest, while the smallest ones observed
are about the size of large rocks.

Because of their small size, they were not called planets but
asteroids. Actually, this is not a very good name since it means
"little stars," but it is still what most people call the tiny planets.

Most of the asteroids swing around the sun in orbits that
lie beween Mars and Jupiter. But some have orbits that carry
them far out from that belt of space. A few swing out as far as
Saturn's orbit. At least one passes closer to the sun than Mercury. Several tiny asteroids pass so close to the earth that they
are known as "Earth-grazers." Apollo, for instance, passes
within 7,000,000 miles of us; Adonis within 1,333,000 miles;
and Hermes within 485,000 miles.

The asteroids are so small that a telescope shows them simply
as points of light, and almost nothing is known about them.
Even so, many people—perhaps including you—have probably
touched pieces of one. Scientists think that some of the meteorites that strike the earth are asteroids. (Others are fragments of

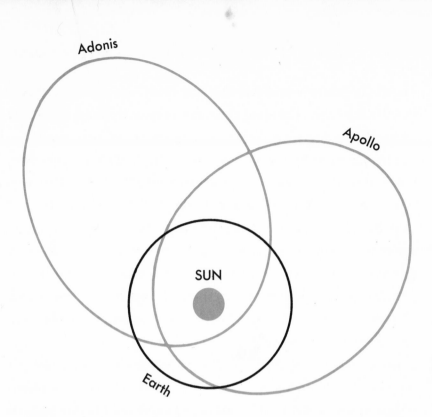

Apollo and Adonis are called "Earth-grazers" because they come so close to us at times.

comets.) Some of these meteorites are made of rock; some of an iron-nickel alloy; and some of both rock and the alloy. To the best of our knowledge the earth is made of these same materials. And if all the planets were born at the same time in the same cloud of dust and gas, then all are probably made of the same materials.

Are the asteroids, then, fragments of a lost planet? Or are they a planet that never formed?

The newest evidence strongly suggests that they are a planet that never formed. This evidence is based on a chemical study of certain elements in meteorites. The study shows that during most of their existence the meteorites remained at a temperature of minus 121 degrees Fahrenheit. This indicates two things:

They have never been closer to the sun than 140 million miles, about the distance of the asteroid belt. Otherwise the sun's rays would have heated them up.

They have never been part of an object with a diameter greater than 100 miles. If they had been part of a large planet, that planet's radioactivity would have heated them up.

If this is so, how can the asteroids be explained?

Some scientists suggest that Jupiter's strong gravitational field prevented a planet from forming in what is now the asteroid belt. Perhaps the material that might have become a planet simply turned into the asteroids. Perhaps it formed a number of small planets that collided with one another and shattered.

However, an earlier theory holds that the asteroids *are* fragments of a lost planet. Long ago, this theory states, a violent accident shattered the planet with a force that must have lighted up the whole solar system. After the accident, a fearsome Age of Meteors began, when gigantic fireballs blasted vast holes in the crust of the earth and other planets.

What could shatter a whole planet into fragments? There are three main theories about this:

(1) The missing planet was destroyed by Jupiter. Scientists know that a large planet can destroy a body that is less massive and less dense than itself. This happens when the smaller body passes into a certain part of the larger planet's gravitational field. There it is torn apart by the force of that field. Perhaps

the missing planet was drawn closer and closer to Jupiter until at last it was shattered.

(2) The missing planet exploded by itself. There is a possibility that radioactivity within the planet created enough pressure to make it explode like a bomb.

(3) It was the victim of a collision. Perhaps it collided with one of Jupiter's moons. Perhaps it collided with something else. One theory supposes that there were two small planets in orbit between Mars and Jupiter and that these two came together in collision.

Precisely what happened remains one of the great mysteries of astronomy. And if mighty Jupiter was the "villain," that planet guards its secret well.

8

Jupiter and Saturn

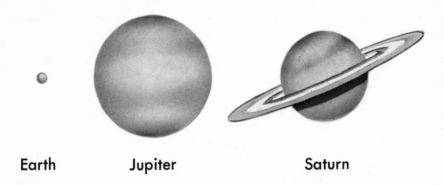

Earth   Jupiter   Saturn

Beyond the asteroids lie four huge and (to us) terrible planets. These are the giants—Jupiter, Saturn, Uranus, and Neptune. The little we know about them shows that they must be almost as hostile to life as the sun itself.

The four inner planets are balls of rock and iron surrounded (except for Mercury) with a little gas. The giant outer planets appear to be mostly atmosphere. They are wrapped in thick, dense layers of gases, some of which are poisonous. Here temperatures are several hundred degrees below zero. On the dark surfaces below, it may be colder yet.

In the beginning, astronomers say, probably all the planets looked like today's giants. But the sun's heat warmed the atmosphere of the inner planets, and most of the gases were driven off. On the outer planets this did not happen. Lying far from the sun, they still hold gases from the cloud out of which the solar system was born.

Astronomers do not agree on what these gases are. One group thinks the atmospheres of the giant planets are mainly hydrogen. Another group thinks they are chiefly methane and ammonia. But whatever they are, the atmospheres are thousands of miles deep. Beneath them may be vast oceans of ice (frozen gases) or of liquid (compressed gases). A solid core of rock and iron may lie beneath the oceans, but no one is sure. The cores may simply be gases under such great pressure that they are as dense as metal.

The outer planet we know best is Jupiter. Named after the king of the gods, Jupiter is also king of the planets. It is a giant among giants, with a diameter almost eleven times that of the earth. Besides being the biggest planet in our solar system, Jupiter is the giant closest to the earth. Its distance from us varies between 369 million and 600 million miles. This may not seem exactly "close," but Jupiter is so big and bright that it can easily be seen without a telescope. Through only a small telescope, it appears as big as the moon does to the unaided eye.

Swinging around a circular orbit, Jupiter takes almost 12 earth years to complete one trip about the sun. But if Jupiter's year is long, its day is short. The big planet rotates once in just under 10 hours. That rapid rate of spinning gives Jupiter the look of a slightly flattened ball.

Like the other giants, Jupiter is far less dense than the small inner planets. The explanation is that the huge disk we see is atmosphere, while the core of the planet is much smaller.

Astronomers suggest that the solid part of Jupiter has a diameter of 37,400 miles—4.7 times as large as the earth's. Covering the core is probably a layer of ice 16,800 miles thick, where huge, jagged ice mountains reach up into the clouds. The atmosphere itself is 7800 miles deep.

The mysterious thing about Jupiter's atmosphere is the way it is marked with broad colored bands and huge colored spots.

These markings have puzzled astronomers ever since they were first seen through a telescope. Some 250 years ago, astronomers thought Jupiter must be red hot and that its bright colors were gases erupting into space. There seemed no other way of explaining Jupiter's brightness and markings.

Today we know that no planet generates its own light. Jupiter shines by light from the sun, and its thick cloud covering makes it a brilliant reflector of light. But astronomers still cannot explain the markings on Jupiter.

The planet's atmosphere is divided into a number of bands, each several thousand miles wide. Sometimes the bands appear as wide belts of pink, tan, yellow, or green-blue. Sometimes they're gray. Generally speaking, the bands have been growing duller in color during the past thirty years. But why they should change color at all, no one knows.

The bands change in other ways, too. Sometimes they shift positions. And their rates of rotation vary. Around Jupiter's equator is a belt 10,000 to 15,000 miles wide; it rotates once every 9 hours and 50 minutes. Other bands take 5 or 6 minutes longer.

In addition to the bands, astronomers have observed light

spots and dark spots and other markings in the atmosphere of Jupiter. All of these also change.

One of the markings is the great Red Spot. When first studied in 1878, it appeared as a red oval, 30,000 miles long and 7000 miles wide. Twelve years later, the Red Spot faded to pink. Some of today's astronomers say it is still a dull pink, while others say it is gray. The Red Spot moves around Jupiter at different speeds, sometimes slowing down and sometimes speeding up. This seems to prove that it cannot be attached to Jupiter's surface; if it were, it would move at a constant speed. The Red Spot may be a solid body of some sort (perhaps a huge cloud of ice) floating in a sea of gas, but no one really knows.

Another strange marking is called the South Tropical Disturbance. Some 45,000 miles long, it moves faster than the Red Spot. But each time it passes the Red Spot (roughly once every two years), the Red Spot is pulled out of shape. No one knows what the South Tropical Disturbance is either.

Quite possibly the markings in Jupiter's atmosphere are related to changes taking place in the hidden core of the planet. Scientists think that the core is hot and molten. If so, volcanic outbursts probably occur, sending up great bursts of hot gases.

The same outbursts may explain some of the radio waves that come from Jupiter—vast bursts of noise that travel some 400 million miles through space and are picked up by radio telescopes on Earth. For some years astronomers thought that the radio waves were caused by lightning during gigantic thunderstorms. Today they are not so sure. Certain bursts of noise always come from the same parts of Jupiter. This suggests that the cause is on the planet's surface.

When it comes to Jupiter's satellites, astronomers find themselves on more familiar ground. As far as we know, Jupiter has twelve moons, most of which are solid bodies.

The four biggest moons—Io, Europa, Ganymede, and Cal-

Jupiter

mean diameter	86,800 miles
mean distance from sun	483,300,000 miles
mean speed of revolution	29,400 miles per hour
length of year	almost 12 earth years
length of day	almost 10 earth hours
gravity	2.64 of earth's
mean temperature (in atmosphere)	−200° F.
moons	12

The Four Big Moons of Jupiter

NAME	DIAMETER IN MILES	MILES FROM JUPITER
Io	2,000	262,000
Europa	1,800	417,000
Ganymede	3,100	666,000
Callisto	2,800	1,170,000

listo—were discovered by Galileo. Io, which is about the size of our moon, appears to be a globe of rock mixed with metal. Some people see it as orange in color; others see it as light yellow or white. Europa appears generally white. At times it seems to have light polar regions and a dark belt circling the equator. Ganymede, which is bigger than Mercury, looks rather like Mars. It has polar caps, a yellow-orange surface marked with dark patches, and some canal-like lines. Though almost as big as Ganymede, Callisto is hard to see. It is considerably farther away from us and a poor reflector of light. In the telescope Callisto appears blue-gray. If this is its true color, then the big moon must be different from the other three. Astronomers suspect that it may be either a solid ball of ice or a ball of rock covered with ice.

For 280 years after Galileo's discovery, astronomers thought of Jupiter as having only four moons. Then, starting in 1892, various astronomers began discovering still more moons circling the giant planet. The eighth additional moon was discovered in 1951.

All eight are small: their diameters range from 20 to 150 miles. One is only 113,000 miles from Jupiter, so close that it may some day be destroyed by the planet's gravitational field. The four farthest out are between 13 million and 14 million miles from Jupiter. They are peculiar because they revolve around Jupiter from east to west. The other eight moons revolve from west to east. Perhaps the four distant moons were asteroids that were captured by Jupiter.

Human explorers will probably never wish to go closer to

Jupiter than its outermost moons. Scientists report that the giant planet is surrounded by a vast sea of deadly radiation. Trapped by Jupiter's magnetic field, this sea is thought to be a million times bigger than the one surrounding Earth and 100 to 1000 times as deadly.

Possibly a way will be found to shield explorers from such radiation. Even so, it's doubtful if they would attempt a landing on Jupiter. In the planet's dense atmosphere they would find frigid temperatures (minus 200 degrees Fahrenheit), poisonous gases, and perhaps violent thunderstorms. On its dark and icy surface, they would be subjected to pressure perhaps 100,000 times as great as Earth's air pressure at sea level. For men, Jupiter is a forbidding and alien world.

Saturn, the slowest-moving planet known in ancient days, was named for the god of time.

In many ways, it is very much like Jupiter. Saturn, too, is an immense planet, probably circled by a sea of deadly radiation. Its surface is hidden from us by a deep, dense atmosphere. The gases in the atmosphere are probably the same as those in Jupiter's. At the bottom of the atmosphere, scientists think, a layer of ice thousands of miles thick encases a solid core. Saturn even shows colored bands and other markings similar to Jupiter's at the top of its atmosphere. Though they are less bright in their coloring, they are probably caused in the same ways as Jupiter's.

Like Jupiter, Saturn has a number of moons. Nine are known, and more may be found.

One of the moons, Titan, may be the largest in our solar system. It is bigger than the planet Mercury and only slightly smaller than Mars. Planet-sized, it has an atmosphere of its own, probably of methane. Titan's surface may be a jungle of methane glaciers. But that is just a scientific guess. The big moon is so far away that it appears in the telescope only as a yellow-orange disk marked with two dark patches.

Almost nothing is known about the other moons of Saturn. The inner ones may be worlds of ice—of frozen water and ammonia. Apart from this, we can only guess that the moon called Phoebe may be an asteroid captured by Saturn. Like the outer moons of Jupiter, Phoebe circles its planet from east to west; Saturn's other moons move from west to east.

But Saturn is not Jupiter's identical twin. Smaller than Jupiter, it is almost twice as far from the sun. For that reason, Saturn is colder and darker. It travels a longer orbit at a slower speed, taking 29½ earth years to circle the sun. But, like Jupiter, Saturn spins very rapidly on its axis. It rotates once in about 10½ hours.

Still, these are minor differences. There is one other thing that not only sets Saturn off from Jupiter but also makes it unique in the solar system. This is Saturn's ring.

Seen with the unaided eye, Saturn appears as a not very bright planet. The ring that makes it both beautiful and spectacular cannot be seen. It takes a telescope to bring the ring into view. And so it happened that Galileo was the first man to see it, though he could not make out what the ring was. As seen through his telescope, Saturn seemed to have a bulging

Observing Saturn through early telescopes, astronomers made drawings such as those below. Stronger telescopes later revealed the rings of Saturn, above.

shape. Galileo at first thought the bulges were caused by two motionless moons. But when the "moons" vanished one night (as the ring sometimes does) he was faced with a mystery he never solved.

It took a much stronger telescope to show astronomers that Saturn was circled by a wide, gleaming ring. Still better telescopes showed that the wide ring consisted of several narrow rings, one within another. The first man to see that was J. D. Cassini of France. In 1675 he clearly saw an outer ring 10,000

As Saturn and Earth move around the s▮

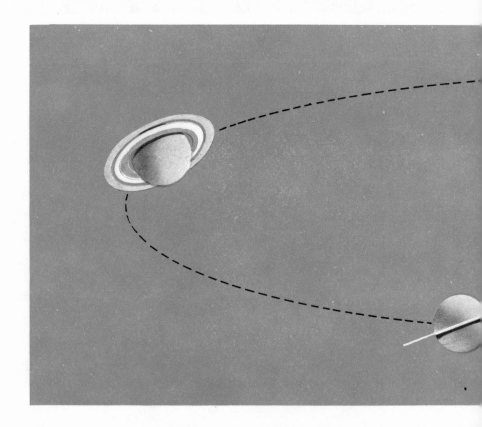

miles wide, then a gap of 1700 miles, then another ring. Later a third ring was found, and there may be still others.

The rings are difficult to see in detail chiefly because they are so far away. Also, since Saturn's axis is tilted at about 27 degrees, we do not always have the same view of them. Sometimes we see the rings from above, sometimes from below. At certain times they face us edge on, and they are so thin that they then vanish from sight.

Once Saturn's rings had been seen, astronomers began to

see Saturn's rings from different angles.

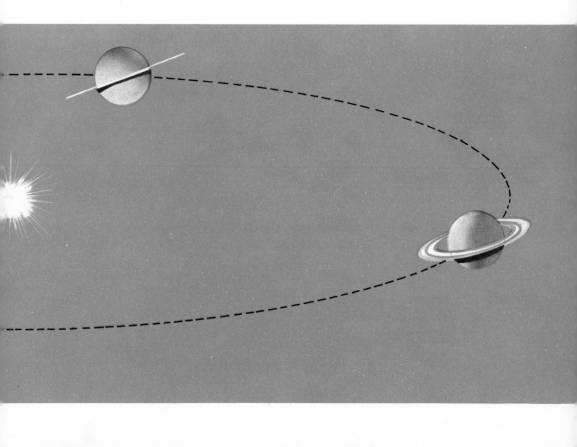

wonder what they were made of. Were they a gas, a solid, or a liquid? The British scientist Clerk Maxwell answered this question in 1857. He showed that the rings could not be either a gas or a liquid, for then they would break apart. Instead, he said, the rings must be composed of a vast number of tiny particles that orbit Saturn.

Today's astronomers agree. They say the particles in the rings are tiny "moons," ranging in size from specks of dust to baseballs. Each particle revolves around Saturn in its own orbit. Since the particles reflect a good deal of light, it's probable that each one is encased in ice or frost. They may even be snowballs formed in some way we do not understand out of water vapor that once surrounded Saturn. However, it's more likely that the particles are tiny pieces of rock covered with ice. Per-

Saturn

mean diameter	71,500 miles
mean distance from sun	886,200,000 miles
mean speed of revolution	21,700 miles per hour
length of year	29½ earth years
length of day	about 10½ earth hours
gravity	1.17 of earth's
mean temperature (in atmosphere)	−240° F.
moons	9 known

haps the rock was left over at the time Saturn formed. Perhaps Saturn once had another satellite that circled closer and closer —into the danger zone of the planet's gravitational field. When the satellite was shattered, the rings formed out of its remains.

If that is so, then the rings spell danger for future space travelers. Not all the particles would be in the rings. Many would be wandering about the planet in odd orbits, forming a swarm of small satellites. Moving at meteor speed, they would wreck any space ship that blundered into their field.

Saturn, one of the most dangerous planets for space travelers, was the outermost planet known to the ancients. Through most of history, men thought that beyond Saturn there was only empty space reaching out to the stars.

But, as we now know, there were more planets sweeping around in lonely paths billions of miles from the sun. Of them, only one can be seen without a telescope. This is Uranus, first of the outermost planets to be discovered.

Uranus

Neptune

Pluto

9

Uranus, Neptune, and Pluto

Earth   Neptune   Uranus   Pluto

The man who discovered Uranus was William Herschel, an English organist who was also an amateur astronomer.

In late winter of 1781, Herschel finished building a new seven-inch reflecting telescope and began to study the stars through it. On the night of March 13, he had his telescope turned on the constellation of Gemini. There to his great surprise he found an extra "star." An excellent astronomer, Herschel was quick to realize that what he had found could not be a star, for it appeared in his telescope as a glowing disk rather than a twinkling point of light. Continuing to observe his find night after night, Herschel discovered that it was moving among the stars of Gemini. Finally he decided that he had discovered a new comet and wrote up a detailed report of his observations.

The report of a new comet excited astronomers all over Europe, and they eagerly trained their telescopes on Herschel's discovery. But the more they studied it, the more they began to wonder if it really was a comet. For one thing, it seemed to be following a nearly circular orbit out beyond Saturn. Finally it became clear that Herschel had discovered not a comet but a planet. In keeping with the names of the other planets, Uranus was called after the god of the sky, perhaps because it was then the most distant known planet.

Uranus lies nearly 2 billion miles from the sun—19 times farther away than the earth. At that great distance, it is difficult to observe. The telescope shows Uranus only as a pale green disk with some fuzzy markings rather like Saturn's. Its brightness seems to vary as it moves in its distant orbit.

Traveling with Uranus are five moons, two of which were discovered by Herschel. They, of course, are even harder to see than their planet. Astronomers think their diameters measure from about 200 miles to 1500 miles. The distances separating them from Uranus range from perhaps 75,000 miles to 365,000 miles.

The diameter of Uranus itself is about 29,400 miles, which makes it the third largest planet in the solar system. It takes 84 earth years to travel round its orbit. But its day, like those of the other giants, is short—10 hours and 45 minutes.

The odd thing about Uranus is the tilt of its axis, with respect to the plane of its orbit. The other planets are tilted somewhere between 3 degrees and 29 degrees. Uranus is tilted 98 degrees.

From our point of view, this means that sometimes we see

Uranus with its north pole pointing at us. At other times we see it with its equatorial belt running up and down instead of across. From the point of view of anyone visiting Uranus, daylight and darkness would be extraordinary. In one hemisphere there would first be a period of daylight lasting 21 earth years. This would be followed by 21 years of twilight. After that would come 21 earth years of darkness, followed by another 21 years of twilight.

However, it is not likely that anyone will spend time on Uranus. The planet's atmosphere seems to consist mainly of poisonous methane gas. Perhaps clouds of ammonia ice crystals float through the atmosphere. The temperature there is minus 310 degrees Fahrenheit. For distant Uranus receives almost no light and heat from the sun.

It was Uranus that led astronomers, sixty-five years later, to

Uranus

mean diameter	29,400 miles
mean distance from sun	1,783,000,000 miles
mean speed of revolution	15,310 miles per hour
length of year	about 84 earth years
length of day	10¾ earth hours
gravity	0.92 of earth's
mean temperature (in atmosphere)	−310° F.
moons	5

Neptune, fourth and last of the giant planets. The discovery came about this way:

By plotting the path of a planet, astronomers can draw up tables that show them exactly where the planet will be at any given time. So, after the discovery of Uranus, they set about plotting its orbit. But for once the method didn't seem to work. Sometimes Uranus turned up ahead of its predicted position; sometimes it was behind.

So astronomers began to think that perhaps another planet lay beyond Uranus. Perhaps its gravitational field was affecting the motion of Uranus. Perhaps that was the explanation of Uranus' odd behavior. For, as astronomers knew, planets do influence one another's motions.

Not until the 1840's did anyone attempt to put that idea to the test. Then, as so often happens in science, two men attacked the problem at the same time without knowing of each other's work. Both solved it. In England, young John C. Adams, only just out of college, proved by mathematics that there must be a planet beyond Uranus and indicated where it might be found. In France, the astronomer Urbain Leverrier also solved the problem.

Both Adams and Leverrier appealed to their fellow astronomers for help in locating the planet.

In England, James Challis searched for the planet during the summer of 1846. Following Adams' directions, he saw the new planet through his telescope—and failed to recognize it.

In the fall of that year, a German astronomer named Johann G. Galle received a letter from Leverrier concerning the unseen

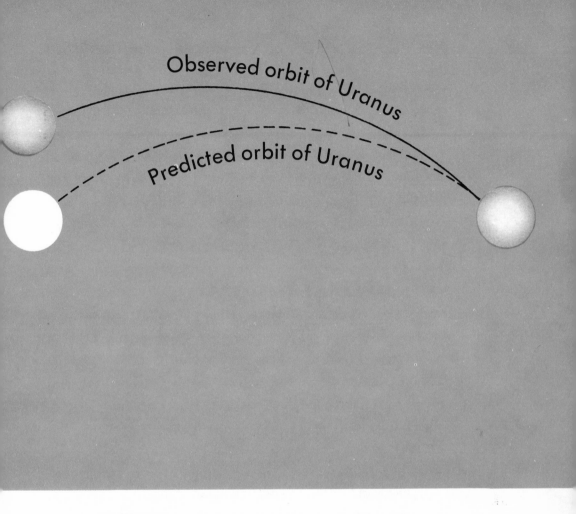

Uranus moved in a different path from the one predicted. This led to the discovery of an outer planet that was affecting Uranus.

planet. The letter arrived on September 23, 1846. Following its directions, Galle found the planet that very night. Since it appeared pale green in color, the new planet was named Neptune, after the god of the sea.

Unlike Uranus, Neptune can be seen only through a telescope. Astronomers report that it has a light band around the equator and that its polar regions are dimmer than the rest of it. That is all the detail that even the most powerful telescopes reveal.

Neptune is the smallest of the giant planets. Its diameter is less than a third of Jupiter's but still three times that of the earth. As the most distant of the giants, it is the slowest-moving. Neptune takes 164¾ earth years to make one trip around the sun. It also spins more slowly than the other big planets. Its day lasts about 15¾ hours.

On Neptune "day" means only the period of rotation, for the planet is nearly 3 billion miles from the sun. At that distance there is hardly any difference between daylight and darkness. Neptune is also an extremely cold world. In its methane and ammonia atmosphere, temperatures hover between 330 and 360 degrees Fahrenheit below zero.

Neptune

mean diameter	28,000 miles
mean distance from sun	2,794,000,000 miles
mean speed of revolution	12,240 miles per hour
length of year	164¾ earth years
length of day	about 15¾ earth hours
gravity	1.12 of earth's
mean temperature (in atmosphere)	−345° F.
moons	2

So far, astronomers have found only two moons circling Neptune. Nereid is tiny, perhaps 200 miles in diameter, and its distance from Neptune is about 3,500,000 miles. Triton, the other, is huge, a giant among moons. Astronomers have not managed to measure it accurately, but they think its diameter is between 3,000 and 5,800 miles. This big moon is only 220,000 miles from Neptune, about the distance of our own moon from Earth. But in the dim light Triton, as seen from its planet, would appear only as a dull gray globe hanging in nearby space.

At first the discovery of Neptune seemed to account nicely for the changes in Uranus' speed. Since Uranus traveled inside Neptune's orbit, there came a time when it overtook its outer neighbor. Approaching, Uranus was pulled along faster by Neptune's gravity. Passing, Uranus was braked and slowed down by Neptune's gravity.

But as time went by, astronomers plotted positions and checked their figures. And Uranus *still* didn't always turn up exactly where it should have been. Was there yet another planet? Was it disturbing Uranus' motion?

Percival Lowell decided that there had to be another planet —an unseen ninth. Like Adams and Leverrier, he sought the planet by using mathematics and based his calculations on what was known about Uranus' orbit. By 1905 he had worked out where Planet X might be found. But he did not publish his prediction until 1915, a year before his death. At Harvard College Observatory another astronomer, W. H. Pickering, also plotted the position of Planet X. He based his figures on how the unseen planet affected Uranus and Neptune. Both Lowell and Pickering believed that Planet X would be found in a certain area of the sky.

Knowing that the planet would be faint and hard to see among the many stars, Lowell searched for it with a telescopic camera. He was looking for a point of light that appeared to move among the fixed stars. But the cameras available were not up to the job. The search had to be abandoned.

Some years later it was taken up again by a young, self-taught astronomer named Clyde Tombaugh. In 1928, using the telescope he had built on his father's farm, Tombaugh spent many nights studying Mars and recording his observations. To see how his drawings compared with those of experts, he sent them to the Lowell Observatory. The director was so impressed with the young man's work that he offered him a job. The job was that of photographic assistant in the search for Planet X.

By the time Tombaugh set to work, the observatory had some new and important equipment. There was a 13-inch telescope with a wide field—one that could cover a large area of sky. There was also a blink microscope. It was used to compare photos taken on successive nights.

Tombaugh's job required him to work with both instruments. With the telescopic camera he photographed the same region of sky several nights apart. With the blink microscope he compared pairs of matched plates. Painstakingly he checked star against star, seeking among many distant points of light the tiny shifting one that might be Planet X. For a year he worked without success.

Then on February 18, 1930, Tombaugh was comparing the plates of January 23 and 29. In them he noted a dot that had shifted its position. Was this Planet X?

It was. The observatory's big telescope showed it as a dim light moving through the distant sky on a steady course. Planet X had been found.

It was called Pluto, after the god of darkness. The name was a fitting choice. The new planet was a dark world. And the first two letters of *Pluto* were the initials of Percival Lowell, the man who first predicted the planet's existence.

Lowell, a brilliant mathematician, had come very close to describing Pluto exactly:

(1) He had predicted a small planet. Pluto is small: its diameter is less than half that of the earth.

(2) He had predicted that Planet X would require 282 years to journey once around its orbit. Pluto makes one revolution in about 248 years.

(3) He had predicted that Planet X would be found 4 billion miles from the sun. Pluto's mean distance is just a little less than that.

Because of its enormous distance from the sun, Pluto travels through endless night, receiving almost no heat or light from the sun. And the sun, as seen from Pluto, would be simply another bright star.

Pluto is so far from the earth that it is extremely difficult to observe. In the most powerful telescope it appears only as a dim yellowish dot. No markings can be seen. If Pluto has moons, astronomers do not see them. Nor can they see Pluto spinning, though they guess it may have a rotation period of 6½ days.

Since Pluto is a poor reflector of light, its surface is probably made up of dark-colored materials. And it must be extremely cold—perhaps minus 375 degrees Fahrenheit.

Beyond these few facts almost nothing is known about Pluto —and some of the "facts" are really scientific guesses. Astronomers are certain only of Pluto's orbit and its smallness.

But that is enough to prove that Pluto is a very odd sort of planet.

For one thing, it is too small to be one of the family of outer planets. In size Pluto resembles the inner planets, which do not have atmospheres thousands of miles deep. It does not seem to belong with the giants.

Yet, small as it is, Pluto appears to influence the motions of both Uranus and Neptune. If it is really doing this, it must be extremely dense with a very strong gravitational field. Its density would have to be 10 times that of the earth—or 5 times that of lead. This is out of keeping with everything known about our solar system.

Then there is Pluto's orbit, which has two odd things about it.

First, it is not in the same plane as the orbits of the other planets. If you could stand on the sun and sight along the orbits of the planets, you would see that they all lined up with one another pretty well—except for Pluto's.

Second, at times Pluto swings inside Neptune's orbit. It moves toward a point where it is 16 million miles nearer to the sun than Neptune is. This is shown in the drawing of the solar system at the beginning of this book.

These facts make some astronomers doubt that Pluto is a true planet. That is, they do not believe that Pluto was born a planet. They think that Pluto was originally one of Neptune's satellites. Escaping from its planet, Pluto began to orbit the sun.

Perhaps there is another giant planet circling in the dark, billions of miles from the sun and as yet undiscovered. But it is much more likely that Neptune is the last of the true planets and that beyond it, at the far reaches of the solar system, there are only comets, Pluto, and possibly a number of other escaped satellites.

Certainly, when seen against the order of the solar system, Pluto does not behave like a true planet. Nor does it fit well into the theory that most astronomers believe explains the birth of the planets.

Pluto

mean diameter	3,600 miles ?
mean distance from sun	3,670,000,000 miles
mean speed of revolution	10,800 miles per hour
length of year	about 248 earth years
length of day	6½ earth days ?
gravity	?
mean temperature	—375° F. ?
moons	?

According to the ancient Egyptians, a heavenly goose laid a daily egg that hatched into the sun.

The Hindus imagined that four elephants standing on a tortoise supported the earth.

The Egyptians believed that stars were lamps hanging from a great ceiling.

10

The Birth of the Planets

In the long history of astronomy, many men have tried to explain how the planets were born. But only in the past two hundred years have there been any scientific theories. Before they were possible, men had to understand the pattern of the solar system.

Its orderliness first came to light in the 1600's and 1700's, through the work of Copernicus, Galileo, Kepler, Newton, and other great scientists. Then astronomers began to see that the sun and planets form one big family. The family is a unit in space. And its members are related in a number of ways. As you remember:

Seen from the north side, all major bodies in the solar system move in a counter-clockwise direction. That is the direction in which the sun and planets rotate on their axes. It is also the direction in which the planets revolve around the sun—all in elliptical orbits.

Except for Pluto's, the orbits of the planets lie on nearly the same plane.

Generally speaking, the planets are separated in an orderly way (Bode's Law).

The planets fall into two classes: small solid bodies and giants wrapped in thick atmospheres.

Such a broad pattern means that all the planets must have been formed at about the same time and in the same way. It means, too, that their birth was somehow related to the sun.

' So all major theories about the birth of the planets stem from one of two basic ideas:

(1) The planets were born in a great cloud of dust and gas, as was the sun.

(2) The planets came directly from the sun.

The first such important theory was published in 1755 by Immanuel Kant, the German philosopher.

According to Kant, the sun and planets had formed out of a huge, thin cloud of dust and gas. Two forces were at work in the cloud. One was the tendency of heavier matter to move toward the cloud's center. The second was the tendency of the cloud to expand. The cloud began to rotate. Gradually, it flattened into a big disk. (The central part of the disk became the sun.)

Within the spinning disk, particles of gas and dust attracted one another. Drawn together, they formed globes—at first very small ones, then larger and larger globes. Finally, matter was packed so tightly around the cores of the globes that they began to give off heat. The globes became huge, hot, molten spheres. Cooling over millions of years, they eventually became the planets and their satellites.

In his own day, Kant's theory did not cause much of a stir among scientists. But today's scientists find much merit in it, except for his explanation of the forces that set the cloud spinning.

Some twenty years later, a very different idea was suggested by a great French scientist, the Comte de Buffon. In 1778 he published his collision theory.

According to this theory, the sun had formed alone; the planets were born much later, when the sun was hit by a comet.

(By "comet" modern scientists think that Buffon probably meant "foreign star.") Because of the collision, billions of tons of matter from the sun were splashed into space. As time went on, this matter collected into globes. The globes contracted and generated heat. Much later they cooled into the planets we know.

Buffon's theory didn't excite much interest either. But the next explanation of the birth of the planets did. It was published in 1796 by a French astronomer named Pierre Simon de Laplace. An expanded and revised version of Kant's idea, it was generally accepted as true for a hundred years.

Laplace imagined that the birth of our solar system began with the tremendous explosion of a star. Exploding, the star expanded, creating a vast fiery mist of gas and dust that reached far out beyond what we know as the limits of the solar system. The fiery mist of gases whirled round its center. After a while, the mist began to cool and contract. Because it was contracting, it spun faster and faster.

The spinning mist threw off great rings of gas. The first ring lay far out—about where the orbit of the farthest-known planet is. The second ring lay within that, the third within the second, and so on.

In time the rings cooled and began to contract, forming more or less solid planets. As they did so, they, too, threw off rings, which became their moons. Meanwhile, the center of the mist had contracted into the glowing globe that became our sun.

Scientists of Laplace's day liked his theory because it seemed to account for the pattern of the solar system. It even explained

why the outer planets were bigger than the inner planets and had more moons: the first few rings thrown off would have been the most massive ones.

Later scientists found two weaknesses in the theory. A major criticism came from Clerk Maxwell, the British scientist who had solved the mystery of Saturn's rings. He said that rings thrown off by the whirling cloud could not have become planets. They would have stayed rings, just as Saturn's ring has stayed a ring. A second criticism has to do with the speeds of rotation in the solar system. Most of the planets rotate faster than the sun. But this would be impossible if the cloud-sun had thrown off ring-planets. There is no way in which the sun could give the planets a faster speed of rotation than it has itself.

So in the late 1800's a number of scientists dropped the Kant-Laplace idea. They turned back to Buffon's theory and began to revise it.

The first important revision was put forward around 1900 by two American scientists, F. R. Moulton, an astronomer, and T. C. Chamberlin, a geologist. Their idea is often called the planetesimal theory; a planetesimal is a tiny planet or a very small heavenly body.

As you may know, all stars travel very rapidly through space. Moulton and Chamberlin suggested that, several billion years ago, another star sped very close to our sun. Its gravitational force raised two great tides, one on either side of the sun. As Star X passed our sun, the top part of a tidal bulge was torn off and hurled into space.

When Star X had passed, some of the material that had been torn loose was drawn back into the sun. But most of it became a great flat ring that circled the sun. Over a period of many years, the gas in the ring cooled and became liquid. Then the liquid changed to small solid masses—the planetesimals. Larger planetesimals kept sweeping up smaller ones, growing and growing. And in this way the planets were formed.

(Naturally, what happened to the sun also happened to Star X. If the theory proved true, Star X would also have a family of planets.)

About eighteen years later, a different version of this theory was worked out by two British scientists, Sir James Jeans and

Harold Jeffreys. In general, they agreed with the two American scientists. But they did not believe that the planets could have formed from planetesimals.

Jeans and Jeffreys said that Star X either had passed very close to the sun or had actually grazed the sun. As a result, matter was pulled out of both stars. It was not a disk but cigar-shaped. That is, it was thickest in the middle and tapered toward the ends. Gradually, the matter in the "cigar" began to solidify into globes. The giant planets formed in the thick section. The small planets formed at the ends.

The Jeans-Jeffreys theory solved certain problems that the Moulton-Chamberlin theory did not. But both shared certain weaknesses. For one thing, they did not really account for the pattern of the solar system. For another, both were based on the very slim chance of a collision between stars. Space is so vast that even a near collision would be a rare event. Jeans himself calculated that one could take place only once in five hundred thousand million million years.

So other scientists continued to work on other theories. One theory suggests that the planets formed out of matter from an exploding star. Perhaps that star had once been our sun's partner in a double-star system. Perhaps our sun and the exploding star were born together in a whole shower of stars.

In a way, that idea is much more probable, for exploding stars are fairly common. But some astronomers rule out these theories. They say the planets could not have formed from matter contained in a star. Such matter would be thousands of degrees hot near the surface. Its swiftly moving molecules would

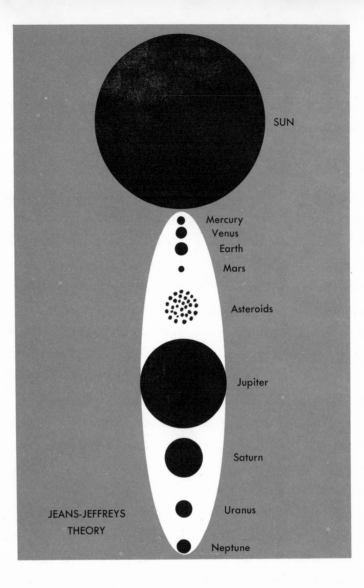

SUN

Mercury
Venus
Earth

Mars

Asteroids

Jupiter

Saturn

JEANS-JEFFREYS
THEORY

Uranus

Neptune

spread out into space and be lost before there was time for planets to form.

Most modern astronomers have now turned back to the very first scientific theory—Kant's. Looked at in the light of modern knowledge, it seems very promising.

For many years, there was one major argument against

Kant's theory: it wouldn't work. What Maxwell had said about Laplace's theory also applied to Kant's: the great flat disk of gas and dust could not turn into planets. It would simply remain a disk.

Today we know this argument does not hold true. The reason has to do with the chemical composition of the universe.

In Maxwell's time, scientists thought the whole universe was made of the same matter we know on earth. That meant the most abundant elements would be oxygen, silicon, iron, and other elements found on the earth. Now scientists know that is not so. The sun and other stars are 99 per cent hydrogen and helium; they contain only 1 per cent of the other elements.

So the great flat disk that formed around the sun must also have been mostly hydrogen and helium. If that is so, the mass of the disk was much greater than Maxwell thought. In a more massive disk, the forces of gravity would have been much stronger. They would have been strong enough to cause the break-up of the disk. Once that happened, planets could have formed.

It was Carl von Weizsäcker, a German scientist, who first showed that Maxwell's argument did not hold up. With that argument destroyed, there was much to be said for Kant's theory. Von Weizsäcker revised it. And his theory has since been revised by Gerard P. Kuiper, George Gamow, and other scientists. Kant's theory, brought up to date, is the one favored by most scientists today. You read a description of it at the beginning of this book.

It supposes that about five billion years ago the sun and planets began to form in a vast, thin-spread cloud of gas and dust.

Under the pressure of starlight and the force of gravity, the cloud particles were drawn toward one another. Slowly, very slowly, the cloud began to condense and contract. As it did so, it started to spin—slowly at first, then faster and faster. Eventually a large part of the cloud collapsed inward. Still contracting and condensing, it began to generate heat and light under enormous pressure. In time this center part of the cloud became our sun.

Meanwhile, another change had taken place in the cloud. The outer parts, spinning faster than the center, had flattened into a disk. Within it, whirlpools formed. They were set in motion by gravitational pull between different parts of the disk.

The dust particles settled toward the centers of the whirlpools. They began to collide. When two particles of the same size collided, they evaporated in the heat developed by the collision. When two particles of different sizes collided, the small one was added to the mass of the large one. In this way, during a few hundred million years, the planets formed.

Each planet was wrapped in a thick envelope of atmosphere. Radiation from the newly glowing sun began to act on the atmospheres, blowing away the lighter gases. The small planets near the sun lost much of the gas that surrounded them. Radiation from the sun was not so great in the case of the giant outer planets. Only a part of their atmospheres escaped. That is why they are still wrapped in clouds of light gases thousands of miles deep.

Most scientists think this new theory is the best yet suggested. It leaves some questions unanswered. But it is in line with what is known about matter in the universe. And it does account for the pattern of the solar system. Born of the same spinning cloud, sun and planets would naturally form the pattern scientists have observed. The only exception is Pluto. But if Pluto was originally a satellite of Neptune, then it is less of a problem. The theory supposes that Neptune is the last of the true planets. Beyond it, the cloud was too thin for a planet to form.

This new theory has not been proved—and may never be proved. Yet there is a good chance that we will one day have a better idea of whether or not it is true.

Scientists believe that new stars are constantly being formed. If they could watch stars forming, it would be like looking back five billion years to the time-misted beginnings of our own solar system.

Perhaps scientists can watch stars forming. Astronomers have found a number of dense, dark clouds in space. These clouds of gas and dust may be stars-in-the-making. Their birth may take a billion years. But watching even a tiny fraction of that time could provide clues to the beginning of our own solar system.

The same clues would help answer a second important question: do many stars have planets?

If planets are born of rare collisions between stars, then there can be only a few families of planets. But if planets are born along with stars, then there must be billions and billions of planets. And, scientists believe, life must exist on some of them.

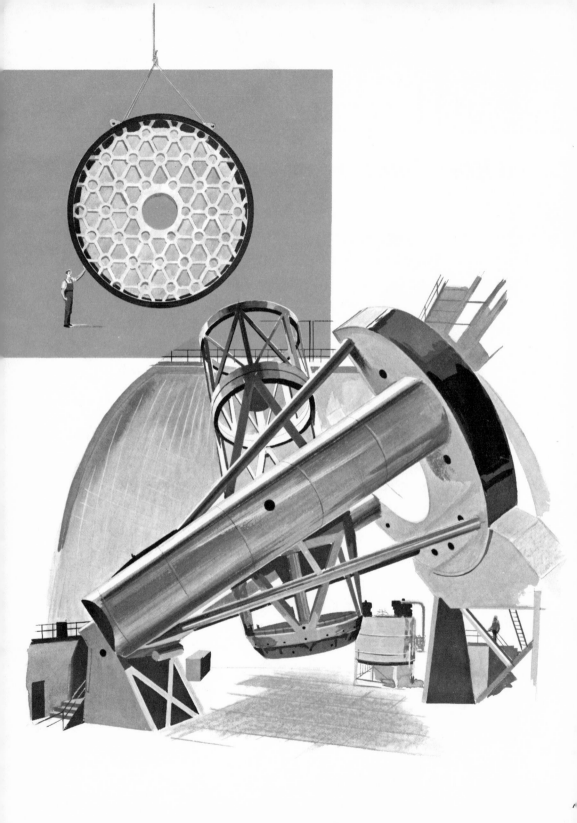

11

Other Suns, Other Planets

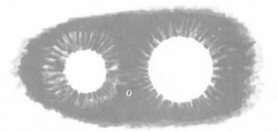

In the constellation of Cygnus there is a star that astronomers have been watching with great interest. Its name is 61 Cygni, which means that it is the 61st star in its constellation.

This is a double star, consisting of two suns. And one of the suns has an invisible companion. The companion circles its sun once every five years at a distance twice that of the earth from our sun. Though the companion cannot be seen, there is evidence it exists. The evidence is the wavy motion of one sun in the double star. Most astronomers think the invisible companion is a giant planet.

This clue—the wavy motion—is the only sign that other solar systems may exist. For the stars are so distant that astronomers cannot hope to see whether or not they have planets. Even so, you would have a very hard time finding a scientist who thought that ours was the only solar system in the universe. Most scientists today believe that there are billions of families of planets. Many are convinced that life exists on a large number of those planets, life rather like the forms we know.

They reason this way:

The whole universe is built from the same elements. All matter, whether simple or complex, is built from these elements. And so far as is known, matter obeys the same laws in every part of the universe. The patterns in our small solar system are part of a pattern so big that the mind can hardly take it in.

We know that our sun was probably born of a cloud of dust and gas, along with its planets. Therefore it is reasonable to believe that other stars were born the same way and that they, too, have planets. And what we know about life on the earth seems to show that life will arise wherever the proper conditions exist.

The "proper conditions" are probably a sun like ours and a planet much like Earth.

Life requires a steady supply of heat and light. This condition rules out the close double stars, triple stars, and clusters of stars. Their planets would move in long orbits hostile to life. It rules out stars that flare up suddenly. In fact, it rules out every kind of star except those single stars that are as steady as our own.

Life requires just the right amount of the right kind of atmosphere. So a life-supporting planet would have to be about the size and weight of Earth. A smaller planet loses its atmosphere; a bigger one may hold too much.

Finally, the planet would have to be just the right distance from its sun. This might be the earth's distance—or it might not. With a weaker sun, the planet would have to be closer. With a stronger one, it would have to be farther away.

Now, suppose that almost every star has a family of planets. How many might support life?

The astronomer first crosses out a majority of the families because they have the wrong kind of stars. (Perhaps half of the stars are doubles, triples, or clusters.) Within the remaining families, he crosses out most of the planets. They are either too close or too far from their suns. Of the planets left, he crosses out all those that are not about the size and weight of the earth. Finally, he points out that the right conditions don't necessarily mean that there is life on a planet. Life may not yet have begun. Or it may have ebbed away. Or the planet may always remain barren for reasons we do not understand.

Perhaps it begins to sound as if there are very few planets where life could exist. In a way, that's true. Life could exist on only a small percentage of the planets—perhaps one in a thousand or one in a million. But there are so many stars that this would still leave a huge number of planets on which life might exist. For the universe is constructed on so vast a scale that it staggers the imagination.

The stars you can see on a clear and moonless night number little more than 2000. They appear very numerous, but they are only a tiny handful of the stars revealed by a telescope. A small, inexpensive telescope shows you 100,000 stars. With the giant 200-inch telescope at Mount Palomar, astronomers can photograph more than a billion stars. And they estimate that in our galaxy alone there are billions and billions of stars.

Our galaxy is the Milky Way, which you know as a faintly glowing band that stretches across the night sky. To the ancient Greeks the band resembled a flow of milk. So they named it the *Galaxy*, which in English means the "Milky Way."

The faintly glowing band consists of stars—a vast multitude of distant stars. Yet it is only the starry edge of our galaxy. The complete Milky Way has the form of a spiral cloud. It includes the stars of our night sky. It includes our sun, which is simply one star in the galaxy. Dust clouds floating in space hide most of the galaxy. But astronomers see enough to know that it must contain about 100 billion stars.

The billions of stars in our own galaxy are only the beginning of the stars in the universe. Some years ago, as telescopes were improving, astronomers found among the stars a number of faintly glowing shapes. Some were round, some oval; others were shaped something like a pinwheel. Astronomers called these *nebulae*, a Latin word for "clouds," because they believed the patches to be clouds of glowing gas. Then, as astronomers got better and better tools to work with, they discovered the truth. Some "nebulae" were not clouds of gas but clouds of stars. Each contained billions of stars and was a complete galaxy.

How many galaxies there are, no one knows. Astronomers estimate that within the range of the 200-inch telescope there are several billion galaxies—each composed of billions of stars.

And there is every reason to think that many more galaxies lie beyond the reach of the telescope.

The stars are so far away that astronomers cannot talk of their distances in miles. Instead they talk of "light years." A light year is the distance that light travels in a year. Since light moves at 186,000 miles a second, a light year equals 5880 billion miles (5,880,000,000,000).

Of all the stars, only our sun is less than a light year away from us. The closest star other than the sun is Alpha Centauri, which is 4⅓ light years away—about 25,000,000,000,000 miles. Rigel, one of the bright stars in Orion, is 540 light years away. The most distant stars we can see with the unaided eye are about 1000 light years away.

Still, compared with the "nebulae," the stars of the Milky Way are our close neighbors. Without a telescope, it is possible to see only one other galaxy—M 31. It is over 2,000,000 light years from us. With the 200-inch telescope, astronomers have seen galaxies 5 billion light years away.

In view of these distances, it's no wonder that astronomers can't see whether other stars have planets. Even if the star nearest us had a planet the size of Jupiter, it would be invisible.

The situation is tantalizing.

The universe may contain billions upon billions of planets where conditions are suitable for life. In the Milky Way alone there may be nearly 50 billion families of planets. At least 100,000 of the families should contain planets where life could exist, and the figure may run much higher.

Yet the planets—if they exist—lie far beyond our vision. Reason and logic say they must exist. But we cannot see them.

Still, scientists feel sure that the planets are there and that some support intelligent life. They feel so sure that they have started to search for signs of that life.

How can they search for life on planets which they cannot see and which may not exist? They can use giant radio telescopes to search for signals from intelligent life on other planets.

Scientists explain the search this way:

Suppose there is life on planets of other solar systems. Some of it will be as advanced as we are, or more advanced. The inhabitants of those planets will also be searching for life in other solar systems. They are probably beaming a message into space, hoping it will be received and answered.

The message would take the form of radio signals. The signals would be simple. But they would have a clearly artificial pattern so that they could be distinguished from other radio noise. For example, they might be based on prime numbers or simple arithmetic.

Today United States astronomers have begun a search for such signals, turning their radio telescopes toward the stars that are nearest us in space. This search is called Project Ozma. It is named for the princess who ruled the imaginary Land of Oz, in the Oz books.

Astronomers admit that Project Ozma is like searching for a needle in a haystack. But, they say, if we try we may fail—or succeed. If we do not try, we are certain to fail.

But if the astronomers do fail, the day will almost certainly come when we know whether or not other stars have planets and life. The knowledge may well come through an invention as yet undreamed of, an invention as important as the telescope.

If other solar systems exist, then men of Earth will seek to communicate with them and perhaps to visit them.

That day lies in the very distant future, for at present the stars are far beyond our grasp. With the kinds of rockets we now know, it would take 28,000 years to reach the nearest stars; to reach stars within a man's lifetime would require speeds comparable to that of light. The rockets we are developing will take us to the planets of our own solar systems, but not beyond.

For that reason, some people will tell you it is foolish to talk of reaching for the stars, trillions of miles away. Perhaps it is foolish. Perhaps it's a waste of time. But it doesn't seem so when you glance back at human history.

A hundred years ago, for example, men could not fly. They knew nothing of atomic energy. Electricity was a laboratory curiosity. And eight thousand years ago man was a wandering hunter who had not yet learned to use fire, tame animals, grow crops, or use metal.

History shows that man is an adventurer. He seeks adventure in the exploration of both unknown lands and unknown ideas. He finds the means to explore by using his brain, the big forebrain that is unique to man among living things on earth. His whole history has consisted of reaching for the "impossible" —and attaining it.

Not long ago, a dreamer who wanted the impossible was said to be "reaching for the moon." Today the moon is within our grasp. And so, seeking other planets, we turn to the stars. They are far beyond our grasp, but in the light of human history it would be foolish not to reach. Even if we fail, we shall still do best with the stars as our goal.

Index

The author

PATRICIA LAUBER, as editor of a science magazine for young people, was caught up in the excitement of man's reach into space with rockets and satellites—devices that will soon turn the ancient science of astronomy into a kind of geography. From her fascination with this subject came *All About the Planets*.

She has written many books of fiction and non-fiction for boys and girls, including *All About the Ice Age*. A graduate of Wellesley College, she lives in New York City.

The illustrator

ARTHUR RENSHAW, after studying at the Art Center School in Los Angeles, worked for two years as a scenic artist for moving pictures. Two of the books he has illustrated are *The Quest of Sir Isaac Newton* and *The Illustrated Book of the Sea*.

Allabout Books

ANIMALS AND PLANTS

All About Animals and Their Young *by Robert M. McClung*
All About Horses *by Marguerite Henry*
All About Dogs *by Carl Burger*
All About Monkeys *by Robert S. Lemmon*
All About Whales *by Roy Chapman Andrews*
All About Fish *by Carl Burger*
All About Birds *by Robert S. Lemmon*
All About the Insect World *by Ferdinand C. Lane*
All About Moths and Butterflies *by Robert S. Lemmon*
All About Snakes *by Bessie M. Hecht*
All About Dinosaurs *by Roy Chapman Andrews*
All About Strange Beasts of the Past *by Roy Chapman Andrews*
All About Strange Beasts of the Present *by Robert S. Lemmon*
All About the Flowering World *by Ferdinand C. Lane*

EARTH SCIENCE

All About the Planet Earth *by Patricia Lauber*
All About Mountains and Mountaineering *by Anne Terry White*
All About Volcanoes and Earthquakes *by Frederick H. Pough*
All About Rocks and Minerals *by Anne Terry White*
All About the Ice Age *by Patricia Lauber*
All About the Weather *by Ivan Ray Tannehill*
All About Maps and Mapmaking *by Susan Marsh*
All About the Sea *by Ferdinand C. Lane*
All About Sailing the Seven Seas *by Ruth Brindze*
All About Undersea Exploration *by Ruth Brindze*
All About Great Rivers of the World *by Anne Terry White*
All About the Jungle *by Armstrong Sperry*
All About the Desert *by Sam and Beryl Epstein*
All About the Arctic and Antarctic *by Armstrong Sperry*

SPACE SCIENCE
All About Satellites and Space Ships *by David Dietz*
All About Rockets and Space Flight *by Harold L. Goodwin*
All About Aviation *by Robert D. Loomis*
All About the Planets *by Patricia Lauber*
All About the Stars *by Anne Terry White*

PHYSICAL SCIENCE
All About the Atom *by Ira M. Freeman*
All About Electricity *by Ira M. Freeman*
All About Radio and Television *by Jack Gould*
All About Engines and Power *by Sam and Beryl Epstein*
All About the Wonders of Chemistry *by Ira M. Freeman*
All About Sound and Ultrasonics *by Ira M. Freeman*

BIOLOGY AND PSYCHOLOGY
All About the Human Body *by Bernard Glemser*
All About the Human Mind *by Robert M. Goldenson*
All About Heredity *by Judith Randal*

GREAT DISCOVERIES
All About Great Medical Discoveries *by David Dietz*
All About Famous Scientific Expeditions *by Raymond P. Holden*
All About Famous Inventors and Their Inventions *by Fletcher Pratt*

MAN'S PAST
All About Prehistoric Cave Men *by Sam and Beryl Epstein*
All About Archaeology *by Anne Terry White*

THE UNITED STATES
All About Our 50 States *by Margaret Ronan*
All About the U.S. Navy *by Edmund L. Castillo*

MUSIC
All About the Symphony Orchestra *by Dorothy Berliner Commins*

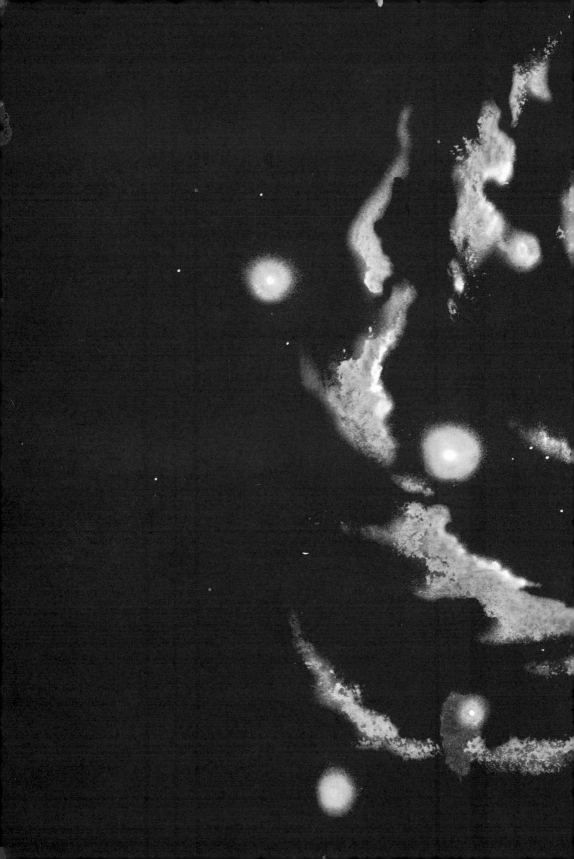